THE CONSCIOUS PARENT'S
GUIDE TO

rails

G

Route # _____
Optional

TO: _____ FRS _____

Code or full name of library

FOR: _____

_____

Code or full name of destination library if different from above

FROM: OLS

_____

NOTES/DATE DUE

_____

THE CONSCIOUS PARENT'S GUIDE TO

COPARENTING

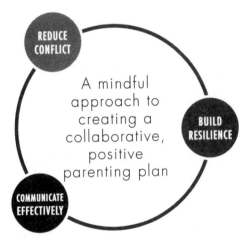

REDUCE CONFLICT

A mindful approach to creating a collaborative, positive parenting plan

BUILD RESILIENCE

COMMUNICATE EFFECTIVELY

Jenna Flowers, PsyD, LMFT

adamsmedia
Avon, Massachusetts

Published by
Adams Media, a division of F+W Media, Inc.
57 Littlefield Street, Avon, MA 02322. U.S.A.
www.adamsmedia.com

Contains material adapted from *The Everything® Guide to Stepparenting* by Erin A. Munroe, LMHC, and Irene S. Levine, PhD, copyright © 2009 by F+W Media, Inc., ISBN 10: 1-60550-055-0, ISBN 13: 978-1-60550-055-3; *The Everything® Parent's Guide to Children and Divorce* by Carl E. Pickhardt, PhD, copyright © 2006 by F+W Media, Inc., ISBN 10: 1-59337-418-6, ISBN 13: 978-1-59337-418-1; and *The Everything® Parent's Guide to Raising Mindful Children* by Jeremy Wardle and Maureen Weinhardt, copyright © 2013 by F+W Media, Inc., ISBN 10: 1-4405-6130-3, ISBN 13: 978-1-4405-6130-6.

ISBN 10: 1-4405-9519-4
ISBN 13: 978-1-4405-9519-6
eISBN 10: 1-4405-9520-8
eISBN 13: 978-1-4405-9520-2

Printed in the United States of America.

10 9 8 7 6 5 4 3 2 1

Library of Congress Cataloging-in-Publication Data
Flowers, Jenna, author.
The conscious parent's guide to coparenting: a mindful approach to creating a collaborative, positive parenting plan / Jenna Flowers.
Avon, Massachusetts: Adams Media, 2016. | Series: The conscious parent's guides.
Includes index.
LCCN 2016002473 (print) | LCCN 2016010514 (ebook) | ISBN
  9781440595196 (pb) | ISBN 1440595194 (pb) | ISBN
  9781440595202 (ebook) | ISBN 1440595208 (ebook)
LCSH: Parenting, Part-time. | Parent and child. | Divorced parents.
  | Children of divorced parents. | BISAC: FAMILY & RELATIONSHIPS / Divorce
  & Separation. | FAMILY & RELATIONSHIPS / Parenting / Stepparenting.
LCC HQ755.8 .F635 2016 (print) | LCC HQ755.8 (ebook) | DDC
  306.874--dc23
LC record available at *http://lccn.loc.gov/2016002473*

Cover design by Alexandra Artiano.

This book is available at quantity discounts for bulk purchases.
For information, please call 1-800-289-0963.

DEDICATION

This book is dedicated to my coparent Erik who makes it possible for me to take on each and every goal I set for myself. To our children Kaylie, Tyson, and Keaton: you are the lights that burn brightly in your father's and my heart. How blessed I feel that our light grows ever brighter together.

To the coparents who have given me the privilege of sitting with them and making sense of their stories. You have taught me so much.

Contents

Acknowledgments

Thank you to Adams Media for giving me the opportunity to write an important book to parents who deserve a voice. To my colleague and confidante Nola Casserly, you have been a wonderful friend and teacher. I am thankful that I could share the essence of our teaching and our hearts for raising children well with coparents. Shelley Volner: thank you for reading my material, editing my thoughts so succinctly, and most importantly for your encouragement in this process. Mike Marshall: thank you for explaining the legal process for coparents with such eloquence that I could actually write about it and share with others. Cheryl Sickels: thank you for educating me further on the legal and personal challenges for coparents. Your time and candor was an invaluable resource. I want to acknowledge all the moms and dads who I encountered in my Conscious Mothering and parenting classes; parents who dared to pursue deeper connections with their children, releasing themselves from old family patterns. Writing this book has been a journey to which all of your stories inspired me and gave me the strength to continue.

Introduction

Parenting is one of the toughest jobs there is. It is a role blanketed in responsibility as well as snuggles, discipline as well as smirks, and stress as well as heart-to-hearts. Parenting is also a mirror reflecting who you are. When issues arise with your children, it's an opportunity to look inward and process your own reactivity. Parenting is a life challenge that can catapult your personal growth even when you don't realize it.

For coparents, parenting may mean something different. The fact that you are reading this book means you either:

O Are separated or divorced with children and you need tools to effectively parent with your ex-spouse.

O Are no longer involved in a relationship with the person you have children with and need to figure out how to effectively parent with each other.

O You and a friend and/or partner have electively decided to have a child together and share in the responsibilities in effectively raising a child.

Regardless of the circumstances, you all have one thing in common: You want to raise your children to the best of your abilities and you have the wisdom to discern that your coparent has to be a part of the equation in some capacity. This is a book for those who recognize that their intimate relationship may no longer work with their parent partner but they have a strong intention to parent well together because it's in the best interest of their child.

This book is a toolbox of discussion topics to consider and plan for when coparenting. You may be reading this book from the perspective that conscious coparenting is solely your responsibility. Conscious coparenting is a mindset and a practice. As you journey through this book, you will enhance your own journey with consciousness. You will increase your knowledge about the developmental stages of your child, about how to be a secure connector, and how to create a successful coparenting relationship. You will read real-life stories of coparents who are pursuing conscious coparenting practices in their homes. Divorce or separation is hard enough on children. Conscious coparenting is the opportunity to rise above the old story of the hurt and pain and create a new story that focuses on raising children with their best interests in mind and consciously working together to achieve this goal. It is my hope that this book brings awareness and healing into your life, and that your family will be touched in powerful and practical ways for the better.

 **CHAPTER 1**

Conscious Parenting

Being a conscious parent is all about building strong, sustainable bonds with your children through mindful living and awareness. Traditional power-based parenting techniques that promote compliance and obedience can disconnect you from your children. Conscious parenting, on the other hand, helps you develop a positive emotional connection with your child. You acknowledge your child's unique self and attempt to empathize with his way of viewing the world. Through empathetic understanding and tolerance, you create a safe environment where you truly hear your child's ideas and concerns. When you find yourself in a stressful situation with your child, rather than reacting with anger or sarcasm, conscious parenting reminds you to take a step back, reflect, and look for a peaceful solution—one that honors your child's individuality and motivations. This approach benefits all children, especially children raised by conscious coparents. Conscious coparents have the challenge of raising securely attached children in two different homes. Conscious coparents understand that even though the intimate relationship between partners was not able to endure, the nurturing and raising of their child, or children, takes precedence.

What Is Conscious Coparenting?

Conscious coparenting is when a coparent consciously chooses awareness and attunement to their child's needs first and collaborates as consciously and effectively as possible with their coparent to raise their child with a secure connection in mind. Both parents desire a secure connection with their child or children, and they understand that the coparenting relationship's primary task is to consider the child's needs and development first before the emotional needs of each parent.

Research on secure attachment shows that children who know how to attach well are happier, more resilient, and physically healthier.

Conscious parenting isn't a set of rules or regulations that you must follow, but rather it is a system of beliefs. Conscious parents engage and connect with their children, using mindful and positive discipline rather than punishment. They try to be present when they're spending time with their children, avoiding distractions like TV and social media. Conscious parents respect their children and accept them as they are. The most important part of conscious parenting is building an emotional connection with your child so you can understand the underlying reasons for behavior.

Conscious parenting is about listening with full attention and embracing a nonjudgmental acceptance of yourself and your child. As you engage in the act of becoming a conscious coparent, you will discover a heightened sense of emotional awareness of yourself and your child; gain a clearer approach to self-regulation in the parenting relationship; and feel a greater compassion for yourself and your child.

Regardless of the circumstances of how you have arrived at coparenting, conscious coparenting supports putting aside all past grievances in order to focus on the main goal, which is to raise a healthy child who is securely attached to both parents. You can pursue this goal and embrace conscious coparenting practices even if your coparent is not in alignment with this practice.

IF YOUR EX IS NOT ON BOARD

After separation or divorce, you may discover a divide in one parent's way of parenting versus the other parent's way of parenting. When this occurs, it can be confusing for the child because the parenting in each of the homes is so different. There are also other challenges such as a lack of consistency or the child getting away with certain things at one parent's house versus the other. As a result, the child may feel caught in the middle, or conversely the parents may find themselves manipulated by the child.

If you and your ex do not agree on parenting methods, there are a few options. One of the more popular books on coparenting suggests treating the coparenting relationship as a business. Raising the child together is a business transaction with each other, and taking the emotionality out of the discussion about the child will help the parent coparent more effectively. There is absolute value to this directive for those parents who have very difficult relationships with their ex-spouses. Additionally, there is another approach that may require more emotional work, but it is much more rewarding. It requires the modeling of secure connecting to your child, and gives your child permission to feel connected to both parents.

The Benefits of Conscious Parenting

Adopting the conscious parent philosophy can relieve your stress and improve your child's self-image. The strong bond built between you and your child, along with your own calm respectful attitude, can help him develop positive behavior patterns. Divorce or separation can have adverse effects on a child's self-esteem, but a conscious coparenting approach can buffer the potential negative effects based on your emotional availability as a parent. Your child will take his cue on how to manage his pain about the transition of family life based on how you are handling your emotions.

Conscious parenting brings with it a number of benefits, including improved communication, stronger relationships, and the feeling of greater happiness and satisfaction in life. Some of these benefits appear more immediately, while others take some time to emerge. The benefits of conscious parenting and mindfulness manifest when you make it a part of your daily life. With practice, conscious parenting becomes an integral part of who and how you are in the world and will in turn become a central part of who your child is as well.

Self-Awareness and Self-Control

One of the initial benefits of conscious parenting that you (and your child) will notice is a heightened awareness of yourself and your inner life, including your emotions, thoughts, and feelings. As you become more aware of these various forces stirring within you, you can begin to watch them rise without being at their mercy. For example, when you are aware that you are becoming angry, you have a choice about whether to act from that anger or attend to that feeling directly. You will start to notice the things that tend to set you off, your "triggers," and you will anticipate your emotions before they have a hold on you.

Mindfulness is the practice of being attentive in every moment and noticing what is taking place inside and outside of you without judgment. It is the practice of purposefully seeing your thoughts, emotions, experiences, and surroundings as they arise. Simply put, mindfulness is the act of paying attention.

As you become more skilled at noticing the thoughts and feelings that arise, you will begin to notice them more quickly, even before they start to affect your actions. This awareness is a powerful tool. It opens up the possibility of saying, "Hey, I'm pretty mad right now . . ." as opposed to yelling at somebody you care about because you were upset about something else. It can do exactly the same thing for your child, helping her to learn to communicate about her feelings rather than just reacting from that place of emotion. As with most things, children learn this best by seeing it modeled by the adults in their lives.

TAKE TIME TO NOTICE

Often, you may notice that your emotions carry with them a sense of urgency. As you feel the impulse to act out arise within you, you will be able to see the forces driving that sense of "I need to do something." They could be, for example, the thoughts that come up as you watch a three-year-old put on her shoes. Your mind might be buzzing with impatience, and the thought "I need to put her shoes on for her because she's taking forever" arises. When you notice this thought, instead of immediately acting on it, you have some room to check in with yourself and act intentionally, instead of just reacting. This practice of noticing creates a certain amount of mental space where you can deal with the thought or feeling itself rather than acting on it.

WELL-BEING

Conscious parents understand that all they do and say over the course of each day matters. It is a sense of the now, being present in the moment without regard or worry for the past or future. When you become more mindful, you may find you become more accepting of the things in life that you can't change and experience less stress. The net result is greater satisfaction and enjoyment of whatever each day has to offer. This sense of well-being offers a satisfaction and contentment in knowing that you are who you are intended to be, doing precisely what you are designed for in the moment.

EMPATHY

The awareness you gain as a conscious parent has the practical purpose of redefining your perception of yourself and your compassionate understanding of your child. When you understand how your child experiences the world and how she learns, you can communicate in ways that really reach her. This largely happens through modeling, or teaching through example. Doing so allows you to pass on the values and lessons that are important to you, regardless of your beliefs. Conscious coparenting strives to honor what both coparents have to teach their child and supports the strengthening of the bonds with both parents.

As human beings, we each possess the tools for contributing something of value. Assess your gifts and talents—those personality traits and skills that make you unique—and determine how to employ them to enhance your parenting. If you take a full accounting of yourself—good, bad, and indifferent—and own the sum total of your individual experience, you are taking the first step toward conscious parenting.

ACCEPTANCE AND VALIDATION

Your child relies upon you and your family to provide a solid foundation of self-esteem. Equipped with a strong sense of self-worth, your child will be better prepared to enter into a life that will likely present many challenges. Much of your time and energy will be spent raising, counseling, and disciplining your child in ways she will understand. It is important to try to equalize those occasions by reinforcing your love and appreciation of her gifts and talents.

Giving Your Child Full Attention

All too often people multitask their way through the day. This is a coping mechanism you have probably developed as a means of juggling the many projects, tasks, errands, and obligations you are responsible for. Although it is a common approach to managing the multiple things you have to do, it splits your attention in ways that distract your mind and actually lessens the quality of your attention. In reality, heavy multitasking causes your work and social interactions to suffer because of how it divides your focus. To avoid this becoming an issue between you and your child (and to make sure you're modeling the kind of focus and engagement you want your child to use as well), make sure to practice engaged listening when you are at home with your family. This means setting aside other distractions, making eye contact, and giving the speaker (in this case, your child) your full attention. Even if you put down what you are doing and look at your child, check in with yourself. Is your mind focusing on what he is saying, or is it still planning, scheduling, remembering, projecting, or worrying? It is very easy to only half-listen, and this can be especially true when it comes to listening to children.

Multitasking is neurologically impossible. When you try to multitask, you actually rapidly switch between tasks. Each time you do so, you lose efficiency and concentration, so stop trying! Do one thing at a time so you can do it with your whole brain, then move on to the next.

The stories your child tells are not always relevant or very interesting to your adult life. The idea behind active listening is not that you suddenly care about what everyone else brought to school for Show and Tell today, it's that you care about your child, and he wants to tell you the funny, strange, or interesting things that he experienced that day. The important part of this interaction is that your child wants to share his joy, curiosity, and interests with you. He wants to interact with you and share parts of himself and his life with you, and this is one of the ways he can do that. Don't miss out on this gift, even if the subject itself bores you. The interest you may develop in these things as you listen to your child talk may surprise you. When a person you love cares about something, it becomes easier to see that "something" through his eyes and come to appreciate it even more.

Important Points to Consider

You want your child to have the best relationship she can have with both parents, and conscious coparenting can provide a secure base to foster secure connections. Here are a few ideas for further reflection:

○ Empathetic understanding and tolerance create a safe environment where your child feels you are truly hearing her ideas and concerns.

○ The most important part of conscious parenting is building an emotional connection with your child so you can understand the underlying reasons for her behavior.

○ When you are at home with your family, engaged listening means setting aside other distractions, making eye contact, and giving your child your full attention.

 **CHAPTER 2**

What Is Conscious Coparenting?

Parents who are coparenting arrive at this practice from a wide array of life experiences. While divorced couples make up the vast majority of coparents, other avenues may lead people to coparenting. Couples who lived together and had children and then decide their relationships no longer align may decide to coparent. There are also elective coparents who find partners to coparent with via friendships and websites because one individual wants to have a child and hasn't found a life partner. Gay and lesbian couples may decide to coparent. Perhaps a couple who is dating discovers the woman is pregnant and decides to coparent the child. Whatever your reason for choosing coparenting, there are a variety of challenges and rewards that go along with this practice.

Challenges of Coparents

Coparenting can present a wide array of challenges. For example, the first challenge for divorced coparents is the realization that they couldn't come to an agreement on certain issues and found that divorcing was the only way to solve the problem. Many challenges often focus around the theme of difference. Different parenting styles, value systems, finances, the ability to spend time with children, how to spend time with children, and expectations can create immense frustrations and disconnects between coparents. In fact, it may be fair to say that when coparents struggle with one another, it may be more about the parent's own issues than what is actually best for the child. When a parent focuses on his or her own needs, it is difficult to remain attuned to the true needs of the child.

Another challenge for coparents can be the prior history they have together that can color their coparenting experiences. If you have negative past associations in your prior relationship, then more than likely you are expecting more of the same behaviors in your coparenting relationship. You may have developed certain habits on how to deal with your coparent. This results in making assumptions that leave little room for change. Typically, once you view a person in a certain way, it is hard to change your perception. This is often why coparents, who have extensive histories of not resolving conflict, continue to struggle, escalating their disputes by using their child as leverage.

The Strengths of Conscious Coparenting

Regardless of how you arrived at coparenting, you have an important choice in how you behave as a coparent. This is where conscious coparenting can help you transform your state of mind of who you want to be and how you want to act. It is ideal if two parents practice conscious coparenting, but one parent can practice it and have effective results. The results are demonstrated in the thriving relationship you have with your child and how emotionally healthy your child thinks, feels, and acts.

Conscious coparenting has added strengths too. For example, when parenting in two different homes, you can potentially set aside a more concentrated time to focus on your child. For parents who have their children full time, it is easier to get caught up in the busyness of home life and take time with their children for granted. Conscious coparents who share the work of parenting can use their nonsupervision time to replenish their inner resources so that when they do spend time with their children, they will feel present and focused. Children who have parents who are physically and emotionally available feel more connected to their parents, have a better understanding of themselves, and have stronger relationships with others.

Conscious coparents can also benefit by having another parent observe the child in a different environment. Sometimes parents who live together begin to defer to one parent's opinion. When the child has two homes, the observations of the child from two different conscious coparents can help the parents understand the child better.

Conscious coparenting is not about being the better parent or the more loved parent by your child. No child wins when only one parent has a connected relationship. If you are truly looking to meet the true emotional needs of your child, then supporting yourself and your coparent's ability to connect with your child is a priority.

In conscious coparenting, awareness of your child happens more organically when you can observe objectively instead of judging your child's behavior in relation to yourself. Your child's behavior is not always about you. All parents can be sensitive to this train of thought because we are often told that children are a reflection of their parents. For coparents, an extra layer of guilt can be created because you are raising your child in two different homes. When this kind of analyzing of your child is happening, conscious awareness is lost because it becomes more about the parent than about the child.

The same is true of analyzing your coparent. If you judge your coparent for character flaws or areas in the prior relationship that still trigger you, this past history and opinion will preoccupy your mind and leave little space for a more evolved relationship. Unprocessed history with your coparent can also be projected onto your relationship with your child and results in decreasing your present awareness.

Putting Your Child's Needs First

Imagine a parenting relationship where both parents are able to put the needs of their child first and collaborate on how to meet those needs to the best of their abilities. As parents, we all have ideas about the best way to parent a child. Conscious coparenting asks the parent to put aside one's own agenda and become lovingly curious about who your child is and what she needs to thrive. Coparents who work together with this intention in mind will have the most fulfillment in their coparenting partnership.

You may be reading this book and thinking this coparenting concept is too altruistic or idealistic. Before you indulge this thought further, think about the power of intentionality and conscious awareness itself. Setting an intention to focus one's mind in a positive direction aids in accomplishing what you have set your mind to achieve. If you are intentional about having a thriving parenting relationship with your coparent, then you will move in that direction. It may not happen quickly but over time and with

Intentions are powerful statements that direct your thoughts toward something you desire to achieve. Write down the specific qualities *you* would like to exhibit in your relationship with your coparent. Once you have identified the qualities, post them somewhere you can see them every day, such as on your bathroom mirror, or set an alarm on your phone reminding you daily. For example, "My intention with _____ is to practice being patient, present, and kind with my words." Daily intention setting reinforces in your brain where you want to put your focused attention.

much repetition and practice, you can foster a coparenting partnership. Consciousness is about being actively aware of how you are behaving or feeling. The application for coparents, then, is setting the intention to practice mindfulness in your parenting and deciding how to approach your coparent with issues about your child. You can change a relationship just by how you choose to consciously interact.

Conscious coparenting will require more effort and repetition initially than parenting from other methods. This is because in conscious coparenting you are focusing on the quality of the relationship between you and your child, as well as on the quality of your relationship with your coparent in support of your child. Enhancing the quality of these relationships takes many repeated efforts to create a new habit. This is particularly so for the parents who are coparenting with ex-partners who were abusive physically, mentally, financially, and emotionally. You may have felt victimized in some capacity in the previous relationship, so to think of continuing a parenting partnership may seem impossible at this point. This may be true for your initial stage in the parenting partnership because you are adjusting to the changes of the relationship itself.

When beginning a new habit, our neural networks in the brain typically need a lot of reinforcement. A research study from the University of London found it takes sixty-six days on average to form a new habit. The study also showed it could take as little as eighteen days, or as much as 256 days based on the context of the circumstances, the habit itself, and the individual. This means coparents should choose one action step in their coparenting they would like to focus on, set a strong intention, and then actively pursue the step daily so the intention becomes a habit.

Give yourself permission to take some time to transition. There is no such thing as the "perfect parent." You will most likely make some mistakes that are potentially hurtful. Rather, strive to be the "good enough parent."

As you read the rest of this book, you will learn tools to help develop your consciousness and move yourself to the change you are seeking. If you set the intention to be more conscious in how you want to parent your child, then you will create the relationship you are seeking. You will encounter the opportunities for growth that are necessary to heal, as well as the communicative tool set you need to work more effectively with your coparent.

Applying the Four S's to Conscious Coparenting

The needs of children are very simple, and even the most well intentioned parents can miss moments to meet those needs. Every child's connection needs typically fall under what neuropsychiatrist Dr. Dan Siegel coined the four S's: safe, secure, seen, and soothed. Let's look at how the four S's apply to coparenting.

SAFE

The experience of being safe takes place for a child on a physical, mental, emotional, and spiritual level. Children need to know that their physical bodies are safe from harm. Safe takes form when coparents provide food and shelter and give the child a sense that they will protect her. The child feels protected and trusts the parent to emotionally hold her.

From a conscious coparenting standpoint, both parents would ideally benefit their child by providing this sense of emotional safety. Divorce or a breakup of the family is a rupture for a child. In order to repair this rupture for your child, consistently reassuring and being available will help repair the lack of emotional safety that your child may be feeling. Some feelings more connected to emotional safety might be abandonment, loneliness, or the fear of being vulnerable.

SECURE

Your child needs to securely attach to you, and ideally to both coparents. You create a secure connection by meeting her emotional needs at least 20–30 percent of the time in your interactions with her. Your children feel secure when you are able to be present and available. Availability isn't always physical presence, but children need both physical presence and emotional presence in order to experience secure connections with their parents. A child may feel some wounds in security after a divorce and transitioning to living between two homes. You can heal this attachment wound by making sure that when you have your shared time, she does not have to share you with distractions, other adult friends, or other entertainment. Moderation with each of these areas is encouraged once you have integrated concentrated time with just you and your child.

Another way to help encourage a more secure connection is to keep your hostility or issues with your ex separate from your time with your child. Too many children feel a need to take sides with one of their parents, and this is unhealthy behavior. A conscious coparent is mindful about how much emotional weight he is placing on his child. Consider what it is like for your child to have to make sense of living with each of her parents in two different homes. Make sure any emotional weight is age appropriate for her and make sure you aren't placing your own emotional baggage on her.

SEEN

Humans have a drive to connect and feeling seen helps us feel more connected. Parents help their children feel more seen when they truly attune to their children's feelings. Parents can attune better when they are self-aware of how they are feeling and thinking, and then acknowledge how their children are feeling too. Feeling seen is a sacred gift parents give their child because it makes the child feel like he matters. To feel seen is to offer your child the experience of "You get me." Conscious coparenting allows your child to be seen by both parents because the time your child receives from both parents stems from the intention to be present and available. When children feel seen, they feel understood.

SOOTHED

Our children's ability to receive comfort when they are upset helps them move to a regulatory state. Some children, because of sensory issues, may take longer to soothe. As coparents, you should try to understand how your child likes to be soothed and use those tools together. Do your best to use the tools of soothing that work for your child, not just the tools that work for you.

The tools of soothing focus on moving your child to self-regulation. Self-regulation occurs when your child accesses the prefrontal and medial corpus callosum and hippocampus parts of the brain. This triad works together to link feelings, thoughts, and senses, and allows calming to reactivate in the brain. You can soothe your children through regulating your own emotional state, voice control, soft eye gaze, gentle touch, reducing your words, and staying present with your child. Reducing words helps your child concentrate on what you really mean rather than being bombarded with a lengthy lecture. Say less so your child can self-regulate. Reducing words also helps the parent to stay calmer because a lengthy lecture can also escalate your emotions, which won't help the situation.

Evaluate how you are doing personally with feeling safe, secure, seen, and soothed. Remember, you need to take adequate care of yourself so you have enough to give to your children.

Some children prefer not to be touched when they are upset. Do your best not to take that personally and/or perceive it as rejection. Just continue to offer your availability to soothe when your child is ready to receive it. The magic of soothing works best when your child is available for comforting. Going against your child's wishes for a hug, or holding her when she does not want to be touched, gives her a message that her body boundaries won't be respected. Typically, children do not want physical touch for comfort because they are so upset that they cannot calm down enough to recognize that comfort would be helpful. Give your child a little space to calm down and then ask again. Use the tonality of your voice and your calm presence to demonstrate soothing if your child does not want a hug or to does not want be held.

Evaluating How Safe, Secure, Seen, and Soothed You and Your Child Feel

Each of these four needs is essential for a child to securely connect with her parents. As a conscious coparent, your ability to assess how safe, secure, seen, and soothed your child feels during your shared time is essential. Your child may need different levels of each, depending on the quantity of time the child has with her parent, the quality of the time, and the history with the parent.

If you find yourself recognizing that you are not attuning well to one of these areas, be compassionate with yourself rather than judgmental. Acknowledgment of an area you would like to change is an important first step, and you can only change if you are willing to accept where you are currently. The second step would be to contemplate a plan to put into practice. Assess how you are doing with helping your child with the four S's:

O How safe do you feel inside? Do you feel whole, healthy, and able to experience positivity and joy regularly?

O How safe do you think your child feels? What are some examples of your child feeling safe or not safe?

O How secure do you think your child feels? What are some examples of your child feeling secure or not secure?

O How seen do you feel right now in your life? Do you have people in your life who really get you? How much time do you get to spend with them? Do you take the time to really identify and process your own feelings and thoughts?

O How seen do you think your child feels by you? What are some examples of your child feeling seen by you? Are there opportunities to grow further in your ability to see your child? How?

O How do you soothe your child? Is your child receptive to your soothing, or does she need something different? What do you notice?

Important Points to Consider

Conscious coparenting is not just a concept, it is a way of being—one where being as available and present with your child as possible is most important. Having a positive relationship with your coparent supports your child's developing self-esteem and knowledge that both of his parents love him. This book has many tools to enhance your coparenting, and by the end of the book, you should have a plan and a conscious awareness that will support your intention. When considering if conscious coparenting is an approach you want to take, consider the following:

- O Conscious coparenting is the ability to live more in the moment with your child. Self-awareness of who you are and how you are behaving becomes a guidepost in your parenting. As a coparent, you are aware that you may have differences of opinion in raising your child, but most importantly, you are putting what is best for your child first.

- O One of the strengths found in coparenting is using your personal time to replenish your reserves so you can be more available to your child during your shared time.

- O The abilities to help your child feel more safe, seen, secure, and soothed are the building blocks for secure attachment. Striving to meet these needs emotionally for your child as conscious coparents will help him be more regulated, resilient, and self-corrective.

CHAPTER 3

Understanding Your Child's Developmental Needs

Part of being a conscious coparent is the ability to identify what your child's needs are. Education on what your child's developmental needs are will help you prepare and normalize. Preparing in advance, whenever possible, will help reduce parental anxiety. For example, knowing that naps are part of the developmental stage, parents should consider this when creating a schedule that allows for these naps so their child is restful and emotionally regulated. Coparents can plan for pickups after naptimes, or early enough prior to a naptime. Coparents can use the developmental stages somewhat as a compass and prepare to work together based on the current needs.

Why Development Stages Are Important

Understanding your child's developmental needs is important. Parents who have not read enough or been taught about developmental stages can often have unrealistic expectations for their children about what is age appropriate, or what their children should already know or not know. For example, parents may have unrealistic expectations about how a child should clean her room at age three, or should need less help with homework at age eight. Every child is different, but developmental stages can provide a framework for what is typically within normal range. If your child doesn't seem to be hitting certain developmental goals, then you can seek guidance from your pediatrician or other parenting resources.

Coparents can use developmental stages to support one another as well as the child. Using the stages to observe your child and then offer feedback to your coparent about what you are noticing can support raising your child in a more united partnership rather than parallel parenting. For the purpose of this book, *parallel parenting* means two parents raising their child as each would prefer without interaction and partnership as parents. As a result, mixed messages occur and there is a lack of consistency for the child because both parents have decided to parent on their own. Children who grow up with parallel parenting often miss out on structure, and typically, one parent may be trying to overcompensate for the other parent's different way of parenting. Coparents are much more effective when a mutual understanding is the foundation. Developmental needs are basic needs all children require in order to feel safe and secure in the world. Let's look at what coparents need to know about the developmental stages.

Birth to Eighteen Months

From birth to eighteen months old, a baby needs maximum comfort with minimum uncertainty to trust herself, others, and her environment. Receiving positive and loving care during the baby stage is critical. Eye contact and touch play important roles in facilitating the baby to trust and to begin to internalize her worthwhileness. If a child does not experience trust with her main caregivers and is constantly frustrated because her needs are not being met, a core belief of worthlessness and mistrust of the world will begin to emerge. The most important relationship for the child is with her primary caregivers.

If you are coparenting a child during this first stage of her life, it is important for the baby to have as much time as possible with both coparents. This is providing both coparents are in a healthy headspace and emotionally available to the child. Conscious coparenting will be easier if you have worked through the emotional baggage from the past relationship. The successful completion of this age stage is that your child believes "the world is a safe place and people are good." If chaos, anger, and caregivers coming in and out of her life is disrupting her life, she may demonstrate more fussiness, difficulty giving eye contact, discomfort with being held, or she may be overly clingy. Conscious parenting means attuning and attending to your child's sensory needs at this developmental stage. If possible, discuss with your coparent how you can best meet these needs during your time with your child.

SOCIAL ENGAGEMENT

Another aspect of this age stage is providing adequate social interaction with face-to-face communication. Conscious coparents see the value in both parents being available and having enough time with their child. Children from birth to five need more face-to-face communication because when caregivers are engaging a baby or toddler, they are wiring the child's brain for connection, and wiring the belief that "you are someone worthwhile, and you can trust that I see you and want to be with you." If both parents are like-minded in offering this message, then you can develop a trust in the parenting partnership that both are conscious

Healthy touch is an important tool when parenting babies. A sweet moment to have with your baby is to lay your baby's belly on top of your belly. The mirror neurons in your body begin to speak to the mirror neurons in your baby's system and can help him feel calmer and even reduce his upset stomach!

of the needs of the child and are putting in the necessary time to nurture the child.

Face-to-face time with your child can look like singing, smiling, little tickles, and games of peek-a-boo. Face-to-face time can also be observing and sharing what you notice. For example, if you see your toddler pick up a ball, and then throw it, you might say enthusiastically, "Adam, you just picked up the blue ball with both hands and threw it to the ground. The ball rolled next to the couch." Little observations provide validation and help our children feel seen.

> Set aside at least ten minutes of every visit with your child to engage in face-to-face time. An ideal system would be ten minutes in the morning, twenty minutes in the afternoon, and ten minutes before bed. During this time, practice engaging through singing a song, reading a baby book, baby massage, or touching games like crisscross applesauce or peek-a-boo, to name a few.

If you and your coparent both have visitation time, consider creating a mobile for each house with pictures of each of you on the mobile. This way your baby or toddler can see your face regularly, even if it is not your visitation time.

RHYTHM

Develop rhythm and predictability in your baby's or toddler's schedule. Predictability helps children feel more secure because they grow accustomed to knowing what's happening next. Conscious coparents who work together to create a similar outline to their day with their child will build an inner clock for the child that helps regulate the time they eat, the time they sleep, and also reduce misbehavior. Each of these areas is an anchored moment to a child's day. Coparents who have a grasp of the importance of anchored moments also help to foster security and safety.

THE VALUE OF SECURITY AND SAFETY

It is important that children in coparenting partnerships regularly feel secure and safe. The reason being is that often when breakups happen, or marriages dissolve, the child's environment has to change and adjusting to this change takes time. In addition, divorced partners are often looking to differentiate themselves from the previous identity they once had in their prior relationship. Part of this differentiation may be the desire to change previous family routines and culture. It's healthy to differentiate oneself, but consider the developmental stage of your child before making any radical changes to your new home life. It's a big transition to sleep in two different homes in the early stage of life, as well as adjusting to the schedule of the shared time arrangement with one caregiver without the presence of the other caregiver, and vice versa. Maintaining a routine for a baby or toddler around the same eating and sleeping schedules helps keep your child healthy and more regulated. Divorcing or breaking up during this age stage does have complications for your child, but continuing a predictable routine will help buffer the circumstances. If both coparents adhere to the same routines, this will also help your child's adjustment to sleeping in two different homes. By being conscious of what your child's sleep, eating, and predictability needs are, you are demonstrating that your child's needs are important to you. Simply put, your child matters to you.

You may not want your coparent to have as much access to your child, but give what is best for your child serious reflection. Coparenting is about sharing time and responsibility for your child. The intention behind coparenting is not single parenting.

If you have reservations because you are concerned about a safety issue for your child, then evaluate if you need to have a further discussion with your coparent. Or is this more of a reactive issue caused by the fact that you don't want to share your child because you are still hurting from the breakup? These are tough questions to ask yourself, but worthwhile answers support a healthier relationship between you, your child, and your coparent.

As conscious coparents of a child during birth to eighteen months old, you want to assure your child that you are confident of her safety and security. Offer statements like "You're okay," "Mommy/Daddy is right here," "I'm coming," or "You are safe with me and you are safe with Daddy," and "She/he will take good care of you."

The Toddler Years: Eighteen Months to Three Years

The toddler years, eighteen months to three years of age, is the developmental stage when a child physically separates from his caregivers and strives to master his physical environment and develop self-esteem in the process. Learning to walk, talk, feed himself, and toilet training are all important milestones during this phase. Each of these milestones should be met with encouragement and compassion from both coparents in order to support the child's beginning efforts at being autonomous. Continued awareness of engaging your child and acknowledging when he masters a milestone is important. Acknowledging does not mean celebrating by buying a toy. It means letting your child know that you recognize that he just accomplished something new. Mutually supporting this stage as coparents supports your child's growing identity because he will learn that both parents believe in his abilities and support him. As your child gains more bodily function control, self-esteem and independence increases. You both can support your child's development by making home environments child safe for movement and exploration. If one parent has a childproofed home and the other parent has a home with many breakables and has to correct the child constantly about touching things, this can create a sense of unsafety in one home. Children at this age cannot decipher how they form their behavior. The thought process sounds more like "I did something bad, so I am bad." This constitutes a message of shame, and children at this age are very sensitive to shame messages because of their newly developing self-esteem. As a conscious parent, you want to do your best to reduce these kinds of messages. When a child feels shame during this stage while potty training, putting on clothes, or other important skills, he will doubt his capabilities.

Conscious coparents are the primary relationships for their child at this time. Spending as much quality time as possible with your child is important. If you are coparenting and it is feasible to work a custody arrangement where there is regular time with both parents during the week, rather than one week on and one week off, then work with your coparent to implement that schedule. The attachment relationships with your child are still forming at this age, so both parent's availability to the child is important. A child's concept of time is very different at this age than when he's older. At age six and up, most children have a more comprehensive understanding of time and days. A child's initial few years are often dreamier and less analytical. The more coparents can support the child's need for regular time with each parent, the better the child's self-esteem will be.

A research study on depression and mothers showed that moms who are stay-at-home moms and are depressed have adverse effects on their children's moods, rather than working moms who come home stimulated from their work and are available to their children. If the time spent at home is fraught with anxiety and preoccupation, then you can't be emotionally available to your child. Take time to get personally healthy so you will be more self-content and have more to give.

LIMIT MEDIA EXPOSURE

At this developmental stage, the less media exposure, the better. Articles, ads, and everything else suggest that parents start their children at an early age with educational videos, television shows, and every electronic device available. It can be common in many homes to use the TV as a babysitter. Work together to decide the amount of TV or media you will allow. Be on the same page when it comes not only to how much TV, but also the types of shows you are comfortable with your child watching. At this age stage, the maximum warranted TV viewing is less than an hour a day. As coparents, if you are mindful about what you are both allowing your child to watch, and for how long, then you create more consistency between the households.

REACTING TO YOUR CHILD'S RISK TAKING

Your child will often look at you and check to see how you feel about what he is thinking of attempting. Your reaction to risk taking encodes in your child's brain associations about risk, safety, good idea, bad idea, and repeat. Each parent has her or his own association with risk taking and typically, boys try riskier things than girls do at earlier ages. Be aware of the need for your child to try new things and be mindful of what your facial expressions and body are saying during the trial. Parents will often differ on the kinds of messages they are giving their child about taking risks. Be mindful to encourage risk within safe parameters that allow a little more challenge, but are also age appropriate.

Providing safe opportunities and toys for walking, running, and climbing during your shared time at this age stage is essential for your child's growing body. This will be covered in a later chapter on rhythm and routine, but consider that your child needs to experience blocks of time at both homes to move his body. This age stage requires children to move, and children will coordinate more effectively as a result.

ENCOURAGE YOUR CHILD TO SLEEP IN HIS OWN BED

This age stage is an excellent time to transition your child to sleeping in his own bed. For families, the positive connections that come out of co-sleeping have typically already happened in the baby stage. For some coparents, over encouragement of their child sleeping in their bed will cause more harm than good. If your child is spending time between two

Your child needs to hear strong messages at this stage. Providing these messages in both homes is ideal, but if it happens in only one home, that's okay. Positive messages that will encourage your child are "You can do it" and "You did it." Affirming messages about your availability to your child sound like "Take my hand . . . I will help you" or "Let's work on this together." Encouragements that affirm your child's development sound like "Look how strong you are getting . . ." or "Now you can sleep in your big boy bed!"

different homes and co-sleeping with one parent and not the other, it presents a confusing message to the child. First, if your child is able to sleep on his own in one house, it proves he is capable of this practice in the other home. Developmentally, sleeping by himself is a healthy sign of individuation.

Second, co-sleeping may be more about meeting the connection needs of the coparent rather than the child. This is not to say that you should never co-sleep with your child. Being flexible when your child has a bad dream and wants to cuddle in, or a Saturday afternoon family nap are all sweet moments. However, co-sleeping can cause confusion and mixed messages for your child, and it is advisable to move toward having your child sleep in his own bed.

POTTY TRAINING

If you are coparenting during potty training, do your best to collaborate with your coparent on the messages and similar practice you are using for elimination. For example, if you have started a gold star chart for potty training, work with your coparent on what you are implementing instead of using two different charts. Keep it simple so your child just has to think about one chart instead of two. Be sure to stay calm when accidents happen and behave neutrally. At this age, play can be enthralling for a child, and sometimes his focus makes him forget to check in with his body cues.

Preschoolers (Three to Five Years Old)

Children at this stage begin to develop confidence in their ability to interest others in joining them in playing and following their creative ideas for play. When a child is successful at getting other children, or caregivers, to play with her, she feels more secure in her ability to survive in the world and take the lead. If children are repeatedly criticized or controlled during this stage, they develop a sense of guilt and believe they should not initiate with others because their ideas are not good enough. During this stage, the most significant relationships are with the child's whole family and preschool.

During this stage, conscious coparents should find time to play with the child during the shared time. Let it be child-led play, meaning you are following your child's directions about what she wants to play. Allowing for twenty minutes of uninterrupted play where you are enthusiastic about what she is interested in encourages your child's self-esteem and inner confidence.

For some parents, child-led play feels difficult. Parents comment that they lose focus, get bored, or don't like what the child wants to play. Remember, the play is for your child, not you. You don't have to like your child's play. Set parameters around the amount of time you can concentrate on the play, for example, ten to twenty minutes. The objective in the play is to be present with your child's imagination. If you are really tired after your workday, it's okay to relax for a little bit before you are ready to play. When your shared time begins, create a routine that allows you to have that playtime.

At the preschool stage, your child needs to hear some messages from both of you: "That's a great idea" or "Okay, I'll pretend to be what you want me to be" or "I would love to play that game with you." This is also a stage where encouragement goes a long way such as, "You always choose a fun game for us to play," or "You invented a great way to cheer up your sister today."

ORGANIZED SPORTS AND COACHING YOUR CHILD

This is the age when children join a soccer or baseball team. Time with your child is not coaching your child's team. If you choose to coach or be a team mom, it's because you want to support your child's budding interest in athletics, learning how to be a part of a team, and you have some coaching ability. As conscious coparents, taking on these roles is part of supporting your child, but it should not be the only way to spend time with him. It will mean more to your child to throw the ball with you rather than watch you coach the whole team. Make time for both play and organized sports at this stage.

School-Age Children (Six to Twelve Years Old)

At this stage, a child is capable of learning, creating, and refining numerous new skills and knowledge. He begins to develop a sense of pride in his accomplishments and in what he is good at. If children are encouraged and acknowledged for their increased skills, they begin to develop confidence in themselves and their ability to achieve goals. Repeatedly criticizing or discouraging a child may make him grow to doubt his abilities and sense of self in the world.

Conscious coparents can help their children at this age stage by doing their best to stay present with their kids during their shared time. It is ideal for both parents to be equally available for homework and encourage their children's developing skills. If the workload falls only on one parent, and the other coparent gets to be more of the fun parent who has outings and activities, this can create resentment for the other parent. Children begin to have antennas for the parent they should go to for different things. Discuss with your coparent what you are both good at with your child and divide the duties up as much as possible. For example, one coparent might have been fine to review homework for the lower grades, but there might be a better point person to take the lead on homework and projects as the homework gets harder. The same is true for following through on a task like learning an instrument. One coparent might have the gift of teaching their child how to discipline himself with daily music practice compared to the other coparent. Recognize your individual strengths as coparents and use them to support your coparenting.

> Here are a few things you might find helpful to say to your child during this stage: "I can see you love to play soccer"; or "Let's finish this session of dance classes, and then you can choose something else you are interested in"; or "I can tell you love to be on stage and you work hard at it."

SUPPORTING THIS STAGE OF DEVELOPMENT

In support of their primary school–age child, coparents need to agree to work with their child to find one activity that he likes and is good at. Learning how to dance, a sport, or music lessons require practice, and both parents need to be supportive of regular practice schedules and lessons. Give your child the choice to continue once the series of lessons or the sport's season is over. As much as possible, stay open to what your child wants to try, and discuss how you both can foster the burgeoning passion your child has discovered. If one coparent feels adamant about quitting or continuing, then take time to discuss this with the other coparent first, and then approach your child with the conclusions. Stopping lessons too early often happens before a child has even had the time to grasp a feeling of competence. This is also the stage where teachers and coaches become important people in your child's community. Both coparents need to support these thriving relationships, but they also need to help the child if they feel a teacher or coach misunderstands him.

Adolescence (Twelve to Eighteen Years Old)

In this stage, children seek to "find their niche" in who they are and where they belong. Remember trying on different hair colors or outfits to see if this was the look/statement you wanted people to see? The purpose of this stage is for adolescents to discover who they are separate from their families. Peer influence plays a huge role in how teens view themselves. Many times, adolescents pull away from their mothers and fathers in an attempt to discover who they are as individuals—separate from their primary family role models. No longer do they want to be "just like mommy or daddy." If a teen is unsuccessful in the many attempts of finding her identity, confusion and upheaval may be intense. If successful, this stage helps an adolescent develop a philosophy of life in terms of value system, faith, and morality. Loyalties to friends and causes often result.

Need an idea on how to check in with your teen? Teens have to eat and they tend to love coffee shops, so make time for coffee or lunch, and check in about what's going on with them. The conversation may be short sentences, and not the most cohesive at times, but it is their attempt at opening up at the level they are comfortable with.

Conscious coparents who break up during this stage need to recognize the potential emotional upheaval that can arise for the teen because of the divorce. To help buffer this time for your child, keep your personal issues about why the marriage ended or the breakup happened to yourselves. Continue to give messages to your teen about being loving and available to talk about her feelings. Be wary of oversharing with your teen because your teen presents as mature, or she tells you that she wants to know. It is unwise to share your personal details with your child because it stunts her emotional growth. It's a great idea to offer individual counseling to your teen so she has a safe place to talk outside of her parents.

The teen years are also a time to embrace what marriage and family therapist Nola Casserly calls the concept of "other mothers." This means accepting that other adults will be influential in your teen's life at this stage, and oftentimes more than you will be. This is a good time to introduce mentors and other family members who your teen trusts. It can be painful when your teen starts to pull away, particularly when a major family transition has occurred, like moving to a separate home or a divorce. It may be hard to categorize your teen's behavior to what is developmentally appropriate and what is because of the divorce.

Coparents should find common ground in their children and make sure that their teens know they care and are available to them. Coparents have an opportunity to spend more time with their teens and foster their own unique relationships with them. Embrace your child's unique dress, thoughts, and personality. Enjoy the changes as much as possible. Use your coparenting relationship during the teen years as a united voice on important boundaries, like alcohol, drugs, and personal and sexual safety.

Ask questions that are open ended and guide your teen to problem solving rather than lecturing or solving it for him.

HOW TO SUPPORT THIS DEVELOPMENTAL STAGE

Coparents can support their teen's stage of development by understanding that individuation is developmental and not a personal criticism. Coparents who can talk with one another about their kids can share and compare stories to help alleviate some of the craziness parents can feel in the teen years. Both parents in both homes should insist on respect, and they should allow for growing differences. Encourage your teen and her friends to gather at both coparent's homes whenever possible. If one home is less convenient, then have that coparent take your child's friends out for pizza. Getting to know your child's friends lets her know that you both appreciate who is important to her.

Important Points to Consider

These are good questions to journal about to further support your growth from this chapter:

- O Consider your child's current stage and think about how you perceive her development.

○ Consider how you and your coparent can further support your child's mastery in her current stage.

○ When thinking about your child's developmental stage, reflect on what was most challenging to you personally. Similar triggers from your own childhood can hijack your parenting when your child reaches that same stage.

○ Notice any developmental tasks that feel underdeveloped in yourself and potentially in your coparent. Consider how you might develop them.

 **CHAPTER 4**

The Goal of Secure Connection: Attachment 101

Many parents who coparent fear that their choice to divorce or separate will have emotional wounds. There is validity to this fear, and many people do have emotional wounds from their parents divorcing. Oftentimes, the people who carry these wounds did not have parents who helped them navigate the emotional terrain they were experiencing when their parents divorced. One of the greatest coping skills in life is being a secure connector. Secure connectors are able to process disappointments, and they have the ability to bounce back in situations like a separation or divorce. It doesn't mean sad or tragic things do not happen to secure connectors, but it does mean a secure connector will have better skills to handle problems. This chapter will explore how coparents can raise secure connectors in two different homes.

What Is Attachment Theory?

Becoming a secure connector originates from the theory of attachment by psychiatrist John Bowlby. Dr. Bowlby grew up in England, and in the Victorian tradition, his main caregiver was a governess. He would only visit with his mother for an hour a day in the afternoon for tea. In medical school, he became interested in the study of relationships. His studies coincided with a period during World War II when English children had to leave their parents in war-torn London and move to the country, and it was then that Bowlby began to analyze how children attach to their parents. He noticed patterns of attachment and developed his theory, which has become widely popular over the last thirty years.

Bowlby suggested that when children are raised to believe their primary caregiver will be available to them, they are less likely to experience fear than those who are raised without this belief. He stated that this belief is formed during the years of infancy through adolescence and that once formed, the belief tended to remain unchanged. He also believed that these expectations are formed directly from experience. For example, the child develops expectations that the caregiver will be responsive to his needs because, in his experience, the caregiver has been responsive in the past. Bowlby believed in four characteristics of attachment:

1. **Proximity Maintenance.** The child desires to be near the people he is attached to.

2. **Safe Haven.** The child feels he can return to the attachment figure for comfort and safety.

3. **Secure Base.** The child views the attachment figure as a base from which he can explore the surrounding environment.

4. **Separation Distress.** The child will experience anxiety if the attachment figure is absent.

This section will educate coparents about attachment styles so you are more aware of your child's attachment, and most importantly your own. You should be aware of your own attachment style because it models

Attachment parenting developed out of John Bowlby's research and was made famous by Dr. William Sears in his books on attachment parenting. There are certain practices of attachment parenting, like wearing your baby or the family bed, but the heart of attachment parenting is that the child deeply bonds to the parents, and there is a high level of trust and respect in the relationship in that the child has a confident healthy sense of self. You can benefit from attachment theory without identifying yourself as an attachment parent.

your connection to your child. Although someone may be attracted to attachment parenting, this does not mean the parent is a secure connector. Remember, one of the goals for a conscious coparent is to be a secure connector regardless of parenting practices.

Secure Connection: The Ideal Attachment Style

John Bowlby discovered a certain type of caregiver relationship that fostered physical and emotional connection. Since Bowlby's original work on attachment, more research has surfaced on securely connected children. A securely connected child feels emotionally seen and heard by her parents. The parent has the ability to emotionally attune to the child's needs and meet the needs in a caring way by focusing as little as 20–30 percent of their time on securing this connection. Securely attached children have a tendency to be well adjusted; express a full range of emotions; present happier and are more confident in their abilities; feel like their thoughts and feelings matter to others; can self-regulate their emotions; and if they do not know how to handle a situation, they can ask for help. A securely connected child trusts that help can be found. Securely connected children are able to create meaningful interpersonal relationships.

> In order to create a secure attachment with your child, you need to emotionally attune just 20–30 percent of the time! For coparents, this may be a guilt-relieving statistic because if you have shared custody, you have enough time with your children to attune to them and make the most of your time together. This will help ensure a healthy bond with your children.

ARE YOU A SECURE CONNECTOR?

Coparents who are coparenting after divorce may be reading this and wondering if they are secure connectors. If you have had a breakup or divorce, it is because there was a disagreement of some kind that was not repairable. The manner in which parents deal with a breakup provides their children with messages about handling relationships. Children primarily learn by modeling, and they need to learn how to securely connect from their main caregivers. If you are not a secure connector, then take the time to better understand how you connect. Heal the relational hurts you have because it will benefit you and your relationship with your child.

> Being a secure connector benefits both parent and child because healthy connection with others helps you experience the vibrancy of living. When parent and child have a secure connection, your child can trust the relational bond that has been created. This bond has a rich legacy into adulthood and the future relationships for your child.

A divorce can be a major trauma for a child, depending on how the parents handled the divorce. Your child may have started out as a secure connector, but then her connection strategy changed because of relational trauma or a repetitive lack of responsiveness from a caregiver. Psychoanalyst and psychology pioneer Melanie Klein once said, "A child's earliest relationships live on within them and become a future template for all relationships in the future."

Research shows us that parents pass down their attachment strategy to their children. If you are a secure connector, then you have an 85 percent chance of passing down the same style of secure attachment. Human brains are wired to attach. We have a deep internal need to connect to others.

The Insecure Attachment Styles

The insecure attachment styles evolve from parenting that lacks the skill to attune to children, foster a sense of safety, offer comfort that children depend on, and build children up to feel confident about who they are. These insecure attachment styles are known as *avoidant* and *ambivalent*. Everyone has a primary attachment style, and attachment usually forms by age three. Attachment strategies can also change depending on the relationship. For example, a child can have a secure connection with his father and an ambivalent relationship with his mother.

Attachment strategy can also change based on later relational trauma. For example, someone can start out as a secure connector and then in his twenties, after multiple ruptures with his parent, become more ambivalent in their relationship. Research also shows that attachment strategies are passed down to the kids, and if an avoidantly-attached parent raised you, you have an 85 percent chance of passing this attachment style down to your child. The good news is that if you take the time to work on your attachment strategy, you can change how you attach. It takes time and a great deal of consciousness, but it is incredibly rewarding and worth the effort.

AVOIDANT CONNECTORS

Avoidant attachment strategy develops out of repeated caregiver experiences where a child is raised with the basic physical needs of food, shelter, and some activity, but the emotional life of the home feels like a dry desert. Emotion is not attuned to, and parents often give dismissing messages such as, "don't feel that way" or "what's wrong with you." Avoidant connectors are often very self-reliant because they felt like they only had themselves to rely on, and at some point, they gave up on their parents meeting their emotional needs. A core belief for the avoidant connector is "Even though I communicate, the world may not understand me or be able to meet my needs."

Avoidant connectors also have a smaller band for emotion. Avoiders feel very little on the whole continuum of emotions from exuberance to utter sadness. In fact, avoiders often have a high pain threshold and have strong relationships with animals more than with people. Typically, avoiders have a hard time pinpointing what they are feeling because a caregiver did not model it for them early on. Conversely, the avoidant connector may feel frustrated or angry about someone else's feelings in a relationship.

About 20 percent of the American population is avoidantly attached. As with all these attachment styles, you can change how you connect if you take the time to develop secure connector skills.

If you are reading this and relate to the avoider, your coparenting might have more messages to your child about being more self-reliant since your child is living in two different homes. Raising self-reliant children has some healthy qualities, but ask yourself if you are insisting on self-reliance over building emotional trust with your child. Kids need a safe place to cry and make sense of their feelings.

Avoider parents feel more comfortable with fixing things rather than listening to feelings, particularly if a child cries or throws tantrums a lot. This kind of behavior may be the result of your child not feeling really heard in the first place, so your child is constantly repeating because he has learned to repeat over and over again in order to get his needs met. (This will be covered more in the emotional attunement chapter.) If you have a tendency to try to fix the problem right away, wait until you have listened really well to your child. As a conscious coparent, take inventory on what you are feeling as you are listening. Even if you have this skill and the other coparent does not, using this method to speak to your child will make an incredible difference in your child's emotional well-being.

If you think your child has avoidant tendencies, you can help repair these by your proactivity to reflect and read your child's emotions. Reflect back what you hear your child say and then read the emotion he was feeling when he said it. Having a feelings and faces chart handy at home can be helpful if you have a child or teen who is not able to pinpoint the feeling. If you feel like you or your coparent's caregiving skills may be at the root or your child's avoidant tendencies, you can find a counselor who offers attachment-based therapy and work on the habits that fostered this attachment style in the first place.

The Adult Attachment Interview (AAI) developed by Mary Main and Erik Hesse (1980s) allowed researchers to predict with 85 percent accuracy the future form of attachment of the subject's child. By interviewing parents using a specific set of questions, they could predict the future attachment status of their children.

AMBIVALENT CONNECTORS

Ambivalent attachment stems from a child who experiences a caregiver who is anxious or preoccupied about being with his child. Ambivalent parents often get preoccupied in work, new relationships, and then when it is more convenient for them, over attune to their children. Ambivalent parents struggle with being consistently available. Therefore, the child has the experience of what it's like to be attuned to, but then the parent's physical and emotional presence in the child's life goes away again. This pushing toward and pulling away experience repeated in the relationship leaves the child thinking, "If I communicate my needs, sometimes they will be met, and sometimes they will not. I get anxious trying to figure out which it will be this time."

Ambivalent connectors have the tendency to idealize and devalue relationships. For example, an ambivalent pleaser may think that someone is the most charming, most ideal mate for her after knowing that person for just a couple of weeks. It is easy for the ambivalent connector to get caught up in the intensity of the experience and mistake the intensity for intimacy. Intimacy takes time, and ambivalent connectors are anxious about how much time things take because they would like to see the need met immediately.

Ultimately, ambivalent connectors have experienced what it's like to connect to another, and there is anxiety about being able to have that connection on an ongoing basis. Ambivalent connectors can also come across as intrusive to others because they love the experience of being intensely connected. The downside is it can be off-putting and cause discomfort for others because the person the ambivalent is trying to connect with may not be ready for that level of connection.

As you become more mindful about your attachment style and the secure connector strategies that you want to embrace, you can change how you connect. That's the power and beauty of your brain! The more you practice building secure connector associations, the more you will behave and feel differently in relationships.

The Two Types of Ambivalent Connection Strategies

For ambivalent connectors, two main connection strategies can develop. The first is the pleaser strategy that believes "If I keep giving the person I love everything they want, then eventually the person will awaken to how worthwhile I am, and I will get my needs met from them." The pleaser strategy puts the ambivalent connector in a state of being the constant giver in the relationship and settling for very little in return. The ambivalent pleaser is also very anxious and preoccupied about other people's problems and comes to the aid of others because her worthwhileness stems from pleasing.

The second ambivalent strategy is to vacillate, which means that when this ambivalent attachment style does not get her needs met, she becomes very angry and lashes out. Ambivalent vacillators are passionate people, which makes them spontaneous, fun, very charming, but also very angry and choleric when they feel rejected, unloved, lonely, and abandoned. The vacillator strategy also tries to have intense fights to see if the other person still cares and is invested in the relationship as much as the ambivalent vacillator is.

Coparents who recognize traits of this attachment style in themselves may deal with more guilt than the other attachment strategies because they worry, and if they are honest with themselves, they are anxious about having a strong bond with their child. Yet, you may be unconsciously pushing away moments with your child where you can be present with him by working too much, overscheduling, getting caught up in dating, or friendships, etc. The belief "Your needs make me feel anxious, and sometimes I know how to meet them and other times I don't" may be prevalent if you really think about it.

Disorganized Strategy

The disorganized strategy occurs when a child is attaching to someone who is frightening to him. This unsolvable dilemma is created in the child because babies have an inborn impulse to connect to someone in order to survive. For the child with disorganized attachment, the child is turning toward the very source of terror he is attempting to escape. This creates an emotional paradox that causes the attachment system to become disorganized and chaotic. Thus, the core belief for the child is "Communicating my needs is frightening and creates an unsolvable terrifying experience."

A child with disorganized attachment has two different strategies to try to get his needs met. The first is the controller strategy that attempts

---

When it comes to the statistics of our nation, here's the breakdown on attachment: 50 percent of Americans are securely attached; 20 percent are avoidantly attached; 20 percent are ambivalently attached; and 5–10 percent have disorganized attachment, but this is hard to verify based on the fact that most disorganized attached people do not receive mental health services.

---

to control as much as possible in order to create a sense of safety for the individual. The controller is often rigid in rule making, and demands may seem unrealistic. The controller's greatest fear is no longer being in control because so much was out of control at some point in his life. The second disorganized attachment strategy is the victim. The victim takes on all the blame and repeatedly feels inadequate, devalued, and worthless. The disorganized strategy overlaps a primary attachment strategy of secure, avoidant, or ambivalent. Thus, if the fearful situation is no longer a factor for the child, then the child's primary strategy will continue to present.

Earned Secure Attachment

After reading each of the insecure attachments, you may be feeling worried about your connection with your child, and your connection with others for that matter. Have no fear; there is hope. The fact that you are invested in becoming a more conscious parent says that you are willing to take the steps necessary to change how you connect if you have insecure connection tendencies. In fact, the Adult Attachment Interview proved that secure attachment can be *earned* when a coherent narrative is developed. A coherent narrative is a life story that is consciously understood or has been made sense of, even if it was not ideal or involved some kind of trauma. Mary Main and Erik Hesse's research proved that if parents are willing to make sense of their childhoods, then they have an 85 percent chance of changing their attachment style. This is a powerful and hope-filled conclusion for coparents all over the world because change is within your hands. You have the power to consciously shift how you perceive relationships and behave based on the depth of understanding you have about your own childhood.

Check out this free attachment style survey at *www.howwelove.com*. This survey will help reveal your attachment tendencies, but it is not a conclusive indicator of your primary attachment style.

Every parent has a primary style of attachment, but there are certain relationships that sometimes bring out different attachment wounds. It is also common for children to have different attachment styles with each of their parents. Don't overly focus on how your coparent needs to change his or her attachment style. Just focus on the kind of attachment relationship you want with your child.

Important Points to Consider

A secure connection with your children is a possibility regardless of how your family is shaped. Coparents who desire to be secure connectors need to consider the following:

○ Your attachment style is the model you use to teach your children how to connect.

○ Secure connectors are the ideal attachment style. Secure connectors are objective, flexible, and perceptive about the feelings and thoughts of others.

○ Avoidant connectors are often dismissive and not perceptive about other people's feelings.

○ Ambivalent connectors are anxious and uncertain in relationships.

○ Disorganized connectors are either highly rigid or chaotic and are often involved in highly toxic and boundary-less relationships.

○ If you have an insecure attachment style, you can work on how you attach and earn secure attachment.

 **CHAPTER 5**

Being a Secure Connector

The previous chapter gave a brief synopsis of the different types of attachment styles. This chapter will go into more detail about how you can be a stronger secure connector. You don't have to stay married to be a secure connector. There are many examples in the world of insecure attached people remaining in unhealthy long-standing relationships. Perhaps as a coparent you came to the conclusion that you could model a healthier connection to your child while living in a home separate from your partner.

Understanding Narratives

Understanding your narrative coherently is an important step in becoming a secure connector. A *narrative* is comprehending how you grew up and how your upbringing influenced your way of connecting to others. Some of you may have had amazing childhoods where your parents were involved in your lives and emotionally understood you. Others may have sad or distressing childhood memories. Regardless, secure connectors take the time to process how their history affects them.

You can process your narrative in therapy, but you can also process it through practicing a healthy connection in relationships with healthy boundaries, a twelve-step program, or self-help and spiritual counseling. It is just important that you talk about it, make sense of it, and then consciously choose to behave differently as you become more aware that other choices are available to you. As you make sense of how your childhood impacted you, you can be more consciously aware of how you behave in your relationship with your child. Knowledge is power when it comes to understanding how you grew up and why you say what you say or do the things you do.

Conscious coparents are willing to do the inner work so they have more emotional availability and presence for their child.

Understanding your narrative does not come easy. In fact, it can be very emotional for people if there is significant trauma or if memories have been intentionally shelved. Conscious coparents are willing to do the inner work so they have more emotional availability and presence with themselves and those they love. For example, say you came from a divorced family and your parents modeled not getting along or having any kind of relationship once divorced. This left you feeling lonely and forgotten, but because you were a survivor, you had forgotten how painful that time was. Cut to being unhappily married and deciding to divorce, but deciding to coparent because you remember how painful it was for you that your parents didn't get along. This history typically has imbedded triggers that may unconsciously undermine your actions because you haven't completely dealt with the pain of your own parent's divorce. It is possible that because you don't have an understanding about how your own parent's divorce impacted you, you might not fully attune to how your own child has been affected by your divorce.

UNDERSTANDING TRAUMA

If you have had traumatic events occur during your marriage, divorce, or earlier in your life, experiencing trauma can have a direct impact on how you handle conflict. The midline structures of the brain, also known as the Mohawk of the brain, process your sense of self. Your middle prefrontal cortex registers sensations of the brain and relays messages from the viscera. When your brain has had previous traumatic experiences, it becomes difficult to register internal states and assess the relevance of incoming information. Thus, you learn to shut down the areas of your brain that create terror. Bessel van der Kolk, in his book *The Body Keeps the Score: Brain, Mind, and Body in the Healing of Trauma*, calls this a "tragic adaptation" as unprocessed trauma deadens your ability to be a self. If you don't have a sense of self, then you lose your sense of direction.

When reflecting on something that is upsetting to you, give yourself a "butterfly hug" by crossing your hands across your shoulders and gently squeezing your shoulders. This helps regulate your system and integrate the processing of your brain's right and left hemispheres.

If you have unresolved trauma that may be impacting your ability to coparent, then take the time to make sense of the trauma so you are more emotionally available for yourself and the relationships you most value. Living life feeling deadened to joy and pleasure is a life devoid of happiness. Actions you can take to help process trauma have to approach trauma on two levels: cognitively processing and body release work. More and more research acknowledges the mind-body connection and using body release work like EMDR therapy, sensorimotor therapy, massage, and yoga therapy to help release trauma.

Understanding Your Coparent's Perspective

It may sound even more difficult to understand your coparent's life story, but this awareness has its advantages. Part of this difficulty could be because of how much hurt you have experienced in the past from your coparent when you were together. These same issues may be trigger issues for you about your coparent. However, you made the choice to live independently. In coparenting, you are continuing a partnership that requires some kind of understanding of each other in order to raise your child.

Being cognizant of your coparent's life story helps you foster compassion for what he has been through. You are parenting with a human being who has had a wide array of experiences that have made him who he is in the world, just like yourself. Both of your parenting relationships will reflect those experiences in some capacity. Rather than judge your coparent, evaluate how you can use these life lessons to enhance your child's understanding of the world and relationships.

Both you and your coparent have the commonality of desiring to be as involved as you can be in the raising of your child. Empathy as a conscious coparent is a tool that will bridge more understanding. It's understandable that you both want to do a good enough job raising your kids in two different homes. Being empathic helps you feel less reactive and reduce defenses.

Advantage 1: Models How to Repair Relationships to Your Child

The first advantage to understanding your coparent is it models repairing relationships to your child, a valuable learning experience after divorce for a child and the parent. The message is even though we are better off living apart, we can demonstrate to our child that we can move forward to best support her development. Children feel more secure when they see their divorced parents having a cordial relationship, and for some a friendship.

Advantage 2: Increases Your Knowledge Base

The second advantage to understanding your coparent is it increases your knowledge base. When you understand more thoroughly why a person thinks the way he does based on how he grew up, you can approach problems differently. This doesn't mean giving the person excuses for not taking responsibility for his actions. It does mean that having a fuller understanding helps you navigate the emotional terrain with your coparent more effectively so your child isn't caught in the middle of issues.

Advantage 3: Helps You Navigate the Emotions of Your Child

Relationship ruptures are going to take place between parents and children frequently. Children have upsetting moments with their other parent; the nonoffending parent sometimes gets involved. Understanding your coparent helps you navigate these conversations with your child. The child may want the other parent to soothe her. Provide soothing and comfort, but look to how your child may be able to repair what took place. Work with your coparent on solutions. If your coparent is too triggered and not able to work it out, then you as the parent-on-hand have to help your child make sense of her feelings. It doesn't mean that you fix the problem between your coparent and child, but you need to be a support to your child and available to help your coparent.

Understanding your narrative will not be the complete end to your healing either. It creates a baseline of understanding as you move into doing the deeper work for you to feel more whole. The deeper work means you are seeking to feel what you need to feel and release the residual pain you may have from your childhood and/or your prior relationship with your coparent. When people continue to hold onto the residual pain from relationships, it takes more energy to hold onto it rather than let it go.

Conscious Coparenting Tools

For a conscious person, compassion is that next step. Compassion about how your coparent is wired based on his own childhood and experiences may help you feel more neutral toward him so you can support a stronger coparenting relationship. Develop the "compassionate observer" part of yourself by understanding that you were doing the best you could with the tools you had at the time, and so was your coparent. Understanding your coparent's narrative never implies doing the emotional work for them. You can't. You are only responsible for yourself and how you feel.

> Humanistic psychology pioneer Carl Rogers once said, "Curious paradox . . . when I accept myself as I am, then I can change."

Self-acceptance has to be a part of how you process your attachment history in order to change it. If you get stuck in becoming defensive and dismiss the past experiences of how it impacted you, or how you behaved impacted other people, then emotional growth will move at an abysmal pace. Accepting your coparent for the person he is will also help free you from who you wanted him to be in your prior relationship. When you fully accept who your coparent is and how he or she behaves, then it is possible to forgive. Forgiveness helps you release yourself from the burden of past hurts that are taking refuge in your mind and heart. This kind of pain can feel like an intruder holding up too much psychic energy until you accept and let it go.

Self-forgiveness is another tool that you can use to release yourself from the judgments you have made about yourself. If you are disappointed with how you have behaved in the past, use your conviction or guilt as a learning opportunity to evaluate what you would do differently next time. Feeling guilt is not inherently a bad thing. If left to linger for long periods, it can lead to feeling shame, and that is more difficult to release. Deal with your personal disappointments by understanding them and working toward forgiving yourself. If you were capable of making a different choice at the time, you would have.

If you want to foster a better coparenting relationship, then try having five positive interactions with your coparent for every negative experience. Neurologically, you are building a stronger neural net that reinforces the positive interaction with your coparent. The repetitive interactions can help change your outlook.

Assessing the Four S's in Your Life

If you had a divorce or breakup from your coparent, more than likely you both were not able to help one another feel safe, secure, seen, and soothed in the relationship. Secure connectors are able to receive experiences of safety, security, feeling seen, and soothed, as well as provide these four experiences in a relationship. Evaluate to see if you are creating these four relationships in your own life, so you can come from this secure base with your child. Rate each statement or question on a scale from one to ten, with ten being very true and one being completely false:

Feeling Safe

O How safe do I feel in my life right now?

O I am living in an environment where I feel reasonably safe.

O My children feel reasonably safe in the home environment I have created.

O I am an emotionally safe person; I am trustworthy, and there is mutual support in my relationships.

O I have emotionally safe relationships; I can share or ask for help.

Feeling Secure

○ How secure do I feel in my life right now?

○ My finances cover my basic needs, savings, and a couple of fun outings a month.

○ I contain any anxiety that I have about money around my children.

Feeling Seen

○ How seen do I currently feel in my life?

○ I have friends who take the time to listen to me.

○ I have one or two friends who are excellent at listening.

○ I have the ability to listen well to people close to me.

○ I am involved in organizations or groups that I care about.

○ I feel purposeful or significant in the work I do.

Feeling Soothed

○ How soothed do I currently feel in my life?

○ I have healthy coping practices to help me increase my mood or take care of my health.

○ I exercise at least three times a week for forty-five minutes.

○ I have someone to talk with when I need comfort.

If you are answering below seven in each of these areas, take the time to figure out a plan to increase feeling better. Secure connectors often know their limits and have a stronger ability to maintain healthy boundaries for themselves. If you have areas that are missing, this leaves you vulnerable to making behavioral choices that can hurt.

Your coparenting relationship affects your child and your relationship with your child. If you aren't taking good care of yourself and perceive your coparent as an emotional trigger, then it is common to become reactive and combative. This is where evaluating how healthy you feel emotionally and physically is important because you are coming from a stronger place when working with your coparent.

Important Points to Consider

Understanding your narrative, and your coparent's narrative, helps you have more compassion. When you act compassionately, you experience your responsiveness to problems as empathic and nonjudgmental. This greatly reduces reactivity with your coparent. Consider the following:

O Understanding how you are wired to connect is vital if you want to be a secure connector with your child.

O Understanding your coparent's attachment style gives you a stronger knowledge base, so you can better support your child's relationship with both coparents.

O Evaluate how you are doing with getting your own needs met. What action steps do you need to take to support yourself in any of the areas?

O Taking the time to heal your own story will help you parent your child. You are the greatest tool you have.

 **CHAPTER 6**

Being Emotionally Available in Two Different Homes

Many coparents worry about missing out on having a healthy attachment with their child if they see her only half the time. As you read this chapter, keep in mind that the amount of time you spend with your child is important, but how present and available you are to your child is the deciding factor on how connected the time feels for parent and child. This includes how to maintain a secure connection when your child is at her other home. Learning how to attune effectively is an important skill for coparents. Cooperating with your coparent during shared times, and offering updates on what you noticed about your child, helps further your attunement. This chapter will cover how to maintain a secure connection when your child is at her other home, as well as checking in with your child as she transitions back to your home.

The Building Blocks of Emotional Attunement

Emotional attunement is vital in teaching your child how to be in touch with his own emotions and for your child to learn how to speak up and share feelings. Author and neuropsychiatrist Dan Siegel once said, "It is through the sharing of emotions that we build connections with others. Communication that involves an awareness of our own emotions, an ability to respectfully share our emotions, and an empathic understanding of our children's emotions lays a foundation that supports the building of lifelong relationships with our children."

Conscious coparents need the ability to emotionally recognize how their child is feeling because if you are a single parent, there is only one caregiver onsite that is able to be physically present for the child. When parents get preoccupied with their own issues, a child feels it and handles the parent's preoccupation in a variety of ways mentioned in Chapter 3.

> As coparents, you both want a secure connection with your child. It is not ideal for your child's feelings to shut down with one parent and turn on with the other.

Some children have a parent who they are closer to and that is normal. Being the same or opposite gender, similar temperaments, and sharing common interests can impact the closeness of the parent-child relationship, as well as how much time is spent together and the quality of that time. Regardless of how close your child is to you, emotional attunement will help your child feel more seen and heard, and it will increase the bond you have with each other.

HOW TO EMOTIONALLY ATTUNE

Emotional attunement is when you respond to your child by first aligning your own internal state with your child's feelings. You match and mirror the child's feelings, reflecting on the child's emotion. You empathize with your child before changing the behavior, fixing, or offering an alternative view. The result is the child feels seen, which helps him regulate his emotions and understand himself better.

Emotional attunement breaks down into the following steps:

1. Step One: Read the emotional state of your child.

2. Step Two: Name the emotional state and mirror back to your child what you see. Notice his nonverbal signals and notice what he is saying through his body language and tonality.

3. Step Three: Acknowledge and comfort.

4. Step Four: Offer help or work to change the behavior or viewpoint.

Step One

In order to read the emotional state of your child, you have to be able to be fully present with what your child is feeling. You can read your child's emotions on two levels: verbal and nonverbal communication. Verbal attuning relies not only on what you are saying, but also on how you are saying it. A parent who really hears what her child is trying to say understands the meaning behind her child's words. The parent must then be mindful of her response. Beginning early with building an emotional vocabulary helps your child identify what he feels so he can share his feelings with you and your coparent.

Nonverbal communication often communicates more than what is actually said. Nonverbal communication refers to your body language, tonality of voice, eye contact, and facial expressions. Reading nonverbal language requires good observation skills. Children who are not overly articulate need to be attuned to what they are feeling, and their words may not be congruent with what their bodies are telling you.

Step Two

Offer your child what Dr. Dan Siegel calls the experience of "feeling felt." This is when you tune in to your child's feelings to identify the feeling. However, as author and psychologist Dr. Tina Payne Bryson says, "Seeing the feeling, and being present to the child's internal experience of emotion, you can mirror to a child what they are feeling without really connecting to what their experience of their feeling is." For example, when a child is whiny or upset after being told he cannot have a cookie, a tired or irritated parent may say with flat intonation, "I know, you're upset. It's okay." The parent has attuned or mirrored back what the child is doing, but the parent's intonation is a clear giveaway that the parent is not truly present with what the child is feeling inside. The experience of feeling seen and felt has not occurred. Rather, once you have a grasp of what is happening in the situation with your child, calmly share what you are noticing with an empathic reflection. This might sound like, "I see you shaking your head and starting to cry. You seem frustrated about having to wait for a cookie for after dinner. Sometimes it feels really hard to wait, huh?" Genuine empathy can really be experienced for a child because it is more than just reflecting back what you see in a rushed tone. Empathy leaves your child feeling really understood.

Step Three

Once you have attuned and helped your child feel felt, offer comfort through listening and healthy touch, like holding your child or giving side hugs. Your child should feel that you acknowledge and understand her feelings.

These steps to effective emotional attunement will encourage stronger emotional bonds with your child. When you trust your attunement skills and the bond you have, you can coparent without the insecurity of your love being replaced or forgotten.

Step Four

Once your child has experienced being attuned to and has come back to a more self-regulated state, ask questions to help your child solve the problem or offer a different viewpoint your child may be open to. The most important factor with this step is that your child is back in a regulated state. You want your child to have ears to hear. This way you can use the situation as a teaching moment. Offer problem-solving suggestions such as, "Let's put the cookie you want for after dinner on a special plate so you know just where it will be waiting for you." A problem-solving question might sound like, "If you were to eat your cookie now, how would that effect your dinner?" Asking open-ended questions helps your child to build his critical thinking skills.

Case Study: Sasha

Sasha was a bright fifteen-year-old girl with a mom and dad who had been coparenting since she was eight years old. Sasha went to see a therapist during her freshman year because she was growing increasingly anxious about spending time at her father's very small loft. Her father had an urban lifestyle of living in an artsy area where he was an artist himself, and he wanted to be a part of the artist scene and bought a loft space to immerse himself. The downside for Sasha was that her dad's space was an open space with the tiniest of bathrooms. It had no privacy for a young woman to bring her toiletries and necessities that a teenage girl requires. She felt anxious about telling her dad because she didn't want to hurt his feelings. She loved her dad very much, but she simply did not feel comfortable staying at his home anymore. After processing the real need for herself, which was that she wanted her privacy acknowledged and respected, she was able to share with her dad that she wanted him to come out for weekly dinners. Sasha also wanted him to make plans to do activities with her on the weekends. Her dad understood and appreciated her telling him.

Maintaining a Secure Connection with Your Child

A secure connection with both parents is really important to your child's development. The amount and quality of time your child has with both of you is vital. Part of being coparents is accepting that you will not always have access to your children when you want because you share their time. For some parents, this may cause anxiety or sadness because they miss spending time with their children. Missing time with your kids is normal, but do your best and don't allow the anxiousness about connecting with your kids get in the way of trusting the connection you already have.

Time with your coparent is equally important for your child. Your child needs ample amounts of time with both parents for healthy development, provided both parents are healthy people. Assuming that you are both healthy individuals working together to raise a well-adjusted child, your child visiting her other parent is an opportunity for you to practice resting in the security of your parent-child relationship. You have to trust that the connection you have with your child is strong and built on a solid foundation. Positive messages your child has from you about spending time with her parent demonstrate your own security in the relationship. It is okay, and it is expected, that she will have to leave you to spend time with your coparent. Your child does not have to worry about how you are doing without her. You don't want your child to have to carry the emotional burden of thinking she has to take care of you.

Children take their cues on how to handle a situation based on how they see the parent emotionally handling the situation.

A SECURE CONNECTION STARTS BEFORE YOU LEAVE THE HOUSE

Maintaining a secure connection begins before your child leaves for her time with her other coparent. A good example is separation anxiety. When a parent frequently calls to check on a child more than required, the parent is giving the message, "I don't trust you when you tell me you are doing okay." Reinforcing this message increases the child's anxiety and then the child starts to present with stomachaches and worries about being separated from her other parent. Show confidence in your child's abilities to handle herself and in looking forward to her time with her coparent. Not only will your child end up appreciating this message, so will your coparent.

WHEN YOUR CHILD IS SPENDING TIME WITH YOUR COPARENT

Respect your child's time with her other parent by not demanding tuck-in phone calls or a daily check-in call during a regular visitation schedule. Coparents who have a policy in place that supports a quick hello every day between homes lets your child know that she can always ask to call or reach out to her parent as needed, but the on-duty coparent is in charge and is the first responder. The time your coparent has with your child is equally important and needs to be nurtured too. During the times your child is on extended visitation, work out a regular Skype call or phone call.

Empathy training: If you have a tendency to call and check on your child frequently during her time with her other parent, think about what it would feel like for you if your coparent called frequently to see how your child was doing while spending time with you.

If you are worried about how your child's visit is going, what are the signs making you feel this way? If your child is showing signs of discomfort every time she visits her other parent, you may need to probe further and seek professional counsel. Look for signs of withdrawal before and after your child returns. Other symptoms are school changes, appetite changes, lethargy, trouble concentrating, aggressiveness, and/or trouble with eye contact.

Using Technology to Connect As Coparents

Technology can enhance your relationship with your kids and coparent by using it to keep in touch about the kids and staying connected with your older children. Ask your coparent if he or she would agree to, within reason, giving each other milestone updates during your shared time. Use technology to share photos or a video at the game. Have your child use video chat if he wants to connect with his parent. If your coparent seems to be intrusive and overuses technology, or asks for too many updates, do what is comfortable for you.

BUYING A PHONE FOR YOUR CHILD

Many parents decide to buy a phone for their child so he has access to either parent. As conscious coparents, please consider where you stand on phone use, screen time, and what is age appropriate for your child. There is so much research on how too much screen time adversely affects children. Too many children have phones and access to technology too early and their minds are not able to comprehend it. If you feel certain a phone is necessary, then purchase a prepaid phone, or a phone with texting and calls only, for children up to age eleven or twelve. After age twelve, place parental controls on your child's phone and look into safeguarding it.

Coparents often purchase phones too early for their kids because they want to be accessible through the phone. Discuss with your coparent what your phone policy will be and make sure Internet safety is a top priority. Try to work out a schedule for calls for early grade-school children rather than introducing a phone.

USING TECHNOLOGY TO CONNECT WITH PARENTS

If your child has social media apps, like Instagram or Facebook, make sure at least one parent is a follower of your teen's postings or has access to what your teen's online behavior is. It is even better if both coparents participate on the site because it adds more accountability to what you expect from your teen. Texting and saying a quick hi is ideal, even when visiting the other coparent, because the teen years are typically the years where teens isolate and connect more with their peers than with parents. Being able to dialogue and give details to each other as coparents helps you both be better parents during your shared time. Relaying critical information about what you may have found on your child's phone, and then working with your coparent to manage the problem, helps to let your child know that both coparents care and will set limits on phone privileges.

Work with your coparent on what you consider the ideal way to relay updates to each other about your child. Initially, if there is a significant

amount of hurt and distrust, there are websites like OurFamilyWizard
.com (*www.ourfamilywizard.com*) available for a fee. Parents use these
sites as a mediator to document requests and facts. Then the information
is returned to the attorneys involved in the divorce proceedings. If you
have a more amicable coparenting relationship, telephone calls and text
messages may be effective ways to correspond.

Case Study: Kelsey

Kelsey had been raised in a coparenting home since she was a baby. In
junior high, she received a phone and discovered apps that enabled her
to chat online anonymously. Kelsey was receiving inappropriate attention
by way of photos and hassles. She thought it was fun and didn't realize
the potential danger she was putting herself in. Kelsey ended up sharing the apps she was using with another friend. This friend looked into it,
and because her mom was regularly checking her phone, she was able to
catch it and she informed Kelsey's mom, Angela, about what she found.
Angela felt shocked and worried for Kelsey. Rather than tackle the problem on her own, Angela reached out to her coparent Chris and included
him. Chris came over that night and Kelsey had a family meeting with her
parents. Chris brought a stack of papers he had downloaded from her conversations online, and both parents shared their deep concern for Kelsey's
safety. They outlined the consequences and watched Kelsey uninstall the
app on her phone. Angela and Chris worked well together in confronting
Kelsey and setting appropriate limits.

Handling the Big Emotions
with Your Child

Children at every stage have big emotions, and coparents need to understand how to support their children with these emotions. Particularly if
there are big feelings connected to divorce or separation, and these feelings create parenting ruptures. Sometimes, dysregulated big feelings are
tantrums. Tantrums are an opportunity to begin teaching children how to
manage these big emotions early in life.

Tantrums between the ages of two to four are developmentally appropriate due to the dominance of right-hemisphere activity and the immaturity of the left-hemisphere function. A two-year-old can be easily set off to have a tantrum because the brain is in an early stage of development in the prefrontal cortex. The prefrontal cortex helps with decision-making and learning. Children need repetition to learn how to problem solve and manage their feelings. Therefore, when the toddler is having a tantrum, the brain is like a boiling teapot of emotion (right hemisphere) with no language or logic (left hemisphere) to communicate or manage the emotional flooding. This is where a parent's support of being their child's prefrontal cortex is so important. You have to help your child enter back into a regulatory state since it is too difficult for the child to do it on his own.

Two kinds of tantrums surface in children. The first is the "little Nero" tantrum. This style of tantrum is a power play for the child; he is not getting his way and he is throwing a tantrum to coerce his parent into giving him what he wants. A perfect example of this is going to a store for house supplies and your child sweetly asking to see the toy department. Since you had extra time and your child asked so nicely, you say yes. Once you get there, your child asks if you will buy him something. You don't think it's appropriate to buy something for him that day, and then the tantrum begins. You might feel embarrassed about the tantrum because it is happening in a public place. A majority of parents feel coerced into buying a toy for their child in order to quiet the behavior. This type of tantrum is the child trying to control the situation and has the potential of making parents feel powerless if they give in. It is during these kinds of tantrums that a parent needs to feel empowered *not* to give in.

The little Nero tantrums can often make parents feel powerless, and you might find yourself giving in to quiet your child and make her happy. Giving in actually reinforces this behavior for the future. Be in it to win it with this kind of tantrum.

Coparents may see little Nero tantrums during their shared time because the child may want to feel more in control since his parent's divorce or separation was out of his control. Children do not have a voice about when parents are no longer together, and it would not be appropriate for children to have a say about their parents staying together. Parents are the adults and decision-makers of their family, not the children. Coparents would be wise to get to the deeper message of frequent little Nero tantrums. If frequent, it may also be a way to get attention if the child is craving more time with the parent.

Coparents may also struggle with guilt about a divorce or separation affecting their child. If so, they are more prone to give in to a little Nero tantrum because they want to see their child happy during their shared time. Guilt is a tough feeling for parents because it has the potential to move into shame and deceive you into thinking you are a bad parent. You may have residual guilt for changing the family dynamic by divorcing, but your job with your child is to coparent to the best of your abilities, not from guilt. If you have a tendency to pacify a tantrum, then process the guilty feelings so they heal. Coparenting from guilt stops you from being fully present with your child. A child who has frequent little Nero tantrums is testing to see who is in control. A major change in the family system can decrease a parent's credibility in the child's eyes. Work on staying consistent with how you manage a little Nero tantrum.

Little Nero tantrums do not mean that you are a bad parent. Little Nero tantrums are common for children regardless of an intact, divorced, or blended family. See the tantrum as an attempt by the child to impolitely assert himself. Look for other opportunities for your child to experience shared power with you that you can say yes to. Do not feel pressured to give into a little Nero tantrum because you will be reinforcing its frequency.

MANAGING THE LITTLE NERO TANTRUM

Oftentimes, if a child is having a tantrum, there is no stopping it. The first step is to get your child to a safe place so she will not harm siblings, or she may need the space to continue the tantrum in privacy. For smaller children, you will have to pick up your child with flailing legs and arms. Few words are best such as saying, "I know sweetie. That was hard," or "Let's get you to a safer space to feel these big feelings." Once in a more conducive environment for the tantrum, offer supportive messages of "Mommy loves you very much. When you are ready to be comforted, let me know. It can't feel good for you to be so upset." Once your child has settled down, process what happened, how your child was feeling, and what your child *really* needed.

Tantrums can be an exhausting experience for the parent. Children can sometimes have frequent tantrums when moving through a developmental stage. Keep consistent with how you handle the tantrums. Most importantly, continue to remind yourself, "This too shall pass."

It's common for parents to react to little Nero tantrums by punishing and continuing to heap on the punishment to stop the tantrum from escalating. This attempt at squashing the tantrum inadvertently escalates it because the child feels more misunderstood, and then he has to have an even bigger reaction to get your attention of how upset he is feeling. When you process what happened with your child after the tantrum, let him know how you will handle the little Nero tantrum the next time, so he is prepared in advance and knows what to expect. Then follow through on what you said.

If your child is prone to little Nero tantrums, setting limits ahead of time is key. Preparing your child in advance by letting him know what you expect of him when entering a store, setting a limit ahead of time on what will be bought, setting limits on toys that will be shared during playdates or with siblings, desserts that will be eaten, and bedtimes that will occur are just a few of the very important areas where children need to know what your expectations are. This helps your child feel more secure because he knows how you will react; and he knows what you expect.

There are seven behaviors to avoid during a tantrum: 1. Avoid punishing. 2. Avoid rewards. 3. Avoid bribes. 4. Avoid placating your child in the situation. 5. Avoid trying to talk your child out of having the tantrum. 6. Avoid leaving the room. 7. Avoid having a tantrum yourself.

TANTRUMS WHEN VISITING THE OTHER PARENT

Tantrums that encompass spending time with another parent could more than likely be little Nero tantrums, but they can also be a symptom of relational stress about the coparenting arrangement, attachment break with one parent, or a fear of separation from another parent. Working with your coparent to help your child's transition to his visit can be helpful on a few levels. The first is that it models to your child that his parents are continuing to work together in his best interests. Children who see their parents continuing to get along after a divorce or separation can feel more secure with their relationships because there is less anxiety for them to carry. They don't have to worry about having to take sides or being caught in the middle. Frequent tantrums during transitional periods may also happen because the child is unconsciously setting up a situation for the coparents who have to work together to care for their child. For the child, there is still a family who is present in his consciousness, even though the family lives in two separate homes. Although you recognized that the living situation was not realistic, finding a way to coparent effectively, and on friendly terms, gives your child the confidence that you both care about him.

Which of your child's emotions is the most difficult for you to tolerate? Reflect on why this may be so. What may support you and your child to enhance emotional development to help reduce tantrums.

An attachment break in the relationship with one coparent may also be the reason for frequent tantrums at visitation. If your child has not seen his parent regularly, then he may feel anxious, sad, and/or withdrawn about initially spending time together. This can happen in parent-child relationships that have the following contexts:

- The parent and child do not have regular visitation arrangements.

- The parent had to be away for legal or personal reasons, such as mental and behavioral health issues.

- The parent's work requires them to travel frequently.

- The child is having a reaction to having to share his shared time with the parent's new relationship or social friendships.

- The time is not quality time spent together.

- Your child is not feeling safe with his parent during their shared time.

This kind of tantrum is called a *distress tantrum*. It requires conscious attention and comfort to the child's feelings and fears. Distressed tantrums occur when a child is in a dysregulated state that can often trigger the darker emotions of shame, deep hurt, and anger. When a child is having a distress tantrum, it is important for the parent to stay close, available, and offer comfort. You may not fully understand why your child is having a distress tantrum, but you can figure it out better when your child is regulated. Offering comfort helps the child regulate and then connect back to his prefrontal cortex, so he can problem solve and feel calmer.

Distress tantrums may occur in coparenting outside of just normal parenting issues if big feelings about divorce or separation have not been addressed for your child. Conscious coparents acknowledge the hurt, fear, and big emotions that can often come with divorce. They are willing to address the big feelings so the child feels comforted and trusts that both parents will still be there for him, even if they are no longer under the same roof.

Whether it is a little Nero tantrum or distress tantrum, the post-dialogue about what occurred is important. It is your teaching moment with your child on how to regulate better for the next time, and how to practice trying a different coping skill.

In a two-year-old, there is very little left-brain hemisphere capacity to regulate the overload of the emotions from the right hemisphere. Let the tantrum pass and then help the child sort things out by using your own logic and language, which she is still developing.

Important Points to Consider

Attuning is an important building block for securely attaching to your child. Coparents can work together to attune to their child in the following ways:

O Conscious coparents practice emotionally attuning to their children because it fosters a secure connection.

O Align with your coparent on how your child will use technology to connect with the other parent. Agree on what is age appropriate.

O Tantrums are a release in a child's body. They happen because your child accumulated tension over the day or weeks and didn't know how to express it except through a tantrum.

O Saying very little during the tantrum helps reduce adding fuel to the fire. You may have to wait for the tantrum to pass and then fill in for the child's left hemisphere.

O Two types of tantrums can occur, a little Nero tantrum and a distress tantrum. Tantrums are more common in earlier childhood, but they can occur even in the teen years.

 **CHAPTER 7**

Aligning on Mutual Values to Raise Your Child

For many coparents, the idea that you have the freedom to raise your children the way you want in your home can feel liberating. For conscious coparents, you have to bring awareness to the following: Is how I am raising my child in my home what is in the best interest of the child or in my best interest? Working together in your parenting partnership to discover what your mutual values are as parents is most helpful in raising a child with similar messages from both homes on the priority issues. The top two priorities in parenting are to protect your child and to promote your child. Coparents may have different approaches about how to pursue this goal, but the intention needs to be clear for your children.

Protecting and Promoting Your Child

The value of protecting and promoting your child can cover a broad range of areas, including physical, financial, mental, emotional, and spiritual protection.

O **Physical:** Conscious coparents need to consider supporting their child's upbringing by both living in reasonably safe environments. When children feel safe, they can express and explore themselves more freely.

O **Financial:** Providing opportunities for enrichment, whether artistic, music lessons, or sports, helps your child see and experience the world differently. Coparents need to be mindful of their child's interests and invest to the extent that they are able when developing the child's interests in one or two different activities.

O **Mental:** Protecting your child from media that is not age appropriate is essential in this day and age, because there is so much material thrown at your child on a regular basis. Protecting your children from pornographic material, overly sexualized preteen and teen shows, and adult day and evening TV programming creates a safer mental environment because your child may not know how to process what is being done or being said on TV or on the computer. Promoting your child's mental strengths through aligning on academic values, enrichment programs, and classes are important to discuss with coparents. Providing encouragement also helps your child think well of himself and is a building block to his self-esteem.

O **Emotional:** Protecting your child emotionally from any relational backlash from the previous relationship you had with your coparent is key. Children feel safer and more secure with parents who emotionally behave as adults, not as equals who the child needs to take care of. Promoting your child emotionally looks like validating his feelings and taking the time to understand them.

O **Spiritual:** Protecting your child spiritually may look like sharing your faith or spirituality in a manner that feels safe and secure.

Have conversations with your child that are age appropriate about your family's perspective about spirituality—provided your child is asking and it is not an intrusive conversation. If your faith or spiritual path is different from your coparent's, be sensitive to sharing what you both believe. Promoting spirituality in a coparenting situation may encourage a relationship with both faiths for a time until your child is a teenager and can come to his own conclusions about what he believes.

Common Values

Having a conversation about what you both think are the important values to instill in your child is a worthwhile conversation for several reasons. First, it helps coparents understand what is important for each parent to teach their child. You get a sense of what your coparent values most in his parenting skills. Secondly, it affirms the lessons you personally want to be mindful of when parenting. Third, discussing what you most value helps you define the commonalities in your parenting. Identifying the commonalities can help bridge any negative relational history in your relationship prior to being coparents.

Common values also give you common ground when you have to discuss issues for your child. Focusing on the values you have in common helps when you are reinforcing something you want your child to understand the importance of. When a child knows that both of her parents want the same thing for her, there is more levity with the subject and less loopholes. A child can't disqualify what one parent is saying when both coparents agree on its importance. For example, say your grade-school daughter comes home with a C on a history test. You have set the rule that studying for tests and working on her grades is important in your home. You tell her that homework and studying has to happen before any kind of TV time or video gaming will take place. Then your child says, "Well, Mom says just do your best. This is my best. You're punishing me." A defensive response from your child could go bad quickly. Having a mutually agreed upon value around homework helps the coparent handle the issue more effectively.

Now imagine two different responses to this scenario:

○ **Response 1:** You have previously spoken to your coparent about how you both intend to handle homework at each other's home. Both of you agreed that homework and checking the work should take place before any other recreational activities. You have put together a proactive plan with your coparent on how to target vulnerable spots, such as helping your child achieve in school. You are both aware that your daughter is not very enthusiastic about school, and she has minimal motivation for putting in greater effort. You both have agreed that working with her to get homework done, checking her work, and creating solid study habits will be important for her in the long run.

    Action: You tell your daughter, "That's true. Your mom wants you to do your best, and so do I. Your schoolwork and doing your best is important to both of us. Whether you are at Mom's house or mine, studying comes first before play. So let's get started."

○ **Response 2:** This situation feels so typical of what you are used to with your ex. Once again, it feels like your daughter's academics are just on your shoulders. You want your child to do her best, but it is so hard to motivate her. Why do you have to be the bad guy and her mom just gets to be her supporter?

    Action: You tell your daughter, "I am not punishing you. I just want you to take your homework and grades more seriously. I can't speak for how your mom handles homework when it's her time, but on my time, we sit down and get things done before playing video games."

Which of these scenarios would feel more effective to you? Both might work in a coparenting situation, but the first scenario demonstrates a conscious coparenting approach. Both parents adhere to a plan about what is going to work best for their child, taking into account the temperament of the child and how to address the situation. Agreeing on a plan and approach ahead of time helps remove the loopholes that children in coparenting situations can sometimes find when their parents are no longer talking to each other. Conscious coparents put aside the personal backstory and focus on caring for their children as proactively as possible so their children receive the love and attention they require.

Using Virtues to Build Character

Virtues are an important way to build character. Common virtues are taught to children through stories as a way to encourage character building, teach life lessons, and develop an internal moral compass. Evaluate what your top five virtues are and why you value them most. Reflect on what your top five challenges are and what makes these particular virtues so challenging. When you reflect on your coparent relationship, consider which of these virtues you have in common with each other.

Ask yourself how you can use the virtues to grow your child's character. Choosing a virtue theme for the week through nighttime stories, or looking for behavior from your child that demonstrates a specific virtue, helps reinforce honorable behavior.

What if you and your coparent do not share the same belief system? Understanding the virtues can provide a common language to discuss the characteristics that you want your child to develop and grow into. Virtues are a great starting point of conversation for coparents who want to process the values they want to teach their children in order to develop their moral compass. The virtues are:

O Assertiveness

O Caring

O Cleanliness

O Compassion

O Confidence

O Consideration

O Courage

O Courtesy

O Creativity

O Detachment

- Determination
- Enthusiasm
- Excellence
- Faithfulness
- Flexibility
- Forgiveness
- Friendliness
- Generosity
- Gentleness
- Helpfulness
- Honesty
- Honor
- Humility
- Idealism
- Joyfulness
- Justice
- Kindness
- Love
- Loyalty
- Mercy
- Moderation
- Modesty
- Obedience
- Orderliness
- Patience
- Peacefulness
- Prayerfulness
- Purposefulness
- Reliability
- Respect
- Responsibility
- Reverence
- Self-discipline
- Service
- Steadfastness
- Tact
- Thankfulness
- Tolerance
- Trust
- Trustworthiness
- Truthfulness
- Unity

USING VIRTUES IN YOUR COPARENTING

Each coparent will have a preference on what they want to instill in their child. Using the virtues as a way to discuss the virtues that your coparent would like to pass down to your child helps set a strong intention with your shared time. When you are thinking about what you would like to teach your child, you see the possibility in the smallest of moments. For example, a mom had shared that she was taking her sons grocery shopping at a bulk foods shop and saw her son just take a treat from one of the bulk food bins. She stopped him from eating it and taught him about taking things without asking, and she asked him what a better approach would be if he wanted a sample. The son found an employee and asked politely if he could try the treat. The grocer said yes.

Virtues are wonderful discussion points if you share the same belief system. They are an even better topic for coparents who don't share the same beliefs. Discussing virtues with your coparent helps define what is important to both parents. When you look at the list of virtues, each characteristic is an incredible trait. No judgment or defensiveness needs to be elicited in a conversation about the virtues. Work with your coparent to understand the importance of this value to both you and your coparent. When a parent is modeling these traits to her child, the child can internalize these traits because he has had firsthand experience from his parents about what it's like to experience the virtues. It is perfectly fine that both coparents focus on certain virtues or values in their individual households. It would be highly supportive for the parents to respect, as much as possible, what they are both trying to teach in their homes without undermining the other parent. For example, if one parent values modesty in how his teenage daughter dresses, and then receives a different message about what she can wear out in public, he/she should be willing to discuss if the mixed messages are creating problems for the child. Another example might be that one parent values orderliness and wants to teach the kids about picking up after themselves by keeping a clean room. Yet the other coparent has a housecleaner who picks up the kid's room for them. Recognizing where you differ in what you value should come first before trying to change your coparent. It is in the differences where you are often using your skills as a conscious coparent.

Once you have discovered where you align, there are often areas where you have a completely different value or opinion than your coparent. These differences can be quite triggering, especially if it is a value you highly regard or disregard. Practicing acceptance for the differences between you and your coparent will help you reduce your triggers. When the difference compromises your child's safety or protection, then you must be proactive to care for your child's welfare.

Aligning on Essential Topics

Making conscious decisions together on healthcare, academics, and spirituality for your child are essential discussions in coparenting. Covering these areas ahead of time in your coparenting relationship is best. For example on the issue of healthcare, you need to decide who will be the primary parent for doctor visits. If both parents are able to take turns and take notes for the other parent to understand any health issues or medication, then you can create a consistent communication around health for your child.

If you and your coparent do not see healthcare similarly, and it is impacting the health and welfare of your child, then a very serious discussion must take place about how you both use healthcare and what your child's needs are. You may need to consult with an attorney or child advocate if necessary.

ACADEMICS

Academics are an area that can put parents at odds, depending on what they each want from an academic environment for their child. Having one parent as the main contact for homework and special projects is ideal, so fewer assignments get lost between two homes. The primary coparent on school assignments needs to update the other coparent if a school assignment needs to be completed during their child's shared time. The value in both parents being involved with homework is that it models that both parents care about their child's academic success. However, there still needs to be a primary parent so no assignments fall through the cracks, or that an assumption that the other parent has handled it doesn't happen.

In many school districts, it is common for parents to have access to grades throughout the semester. This can be helpful because you know how your child is doing currently at school and if there are classes that need more attention. The downside is that for some parents it can be compulsive. To inquire with your child about every single grade makes your child feel like he is being micromanaged, and ultimately, your child needs to be in charge and take responsibility for his academic success.

The social support at a school is just as important, and coparents need to evaluate what their child needs most out of an academic program. If you have a highly intelligent child who needs more challenges, then pursuing a program that includes a rigorous curriculum may be what your child needs. If your child is very social, then settling into a school with very small class sizes may not be a good fit. You may live near a public school that is not an ideal learning environment for your child and need to transfer. Be willing to have the conversation so you and your coparent can figure out a solution that best fits the needs of your child, and you can financially sustain it. A child's academic environment is very important to discuss because so much of his development takes place in the school setting. You don't want to have to move your child from his school environment unless it is necessary.

When Coparenting Becomes Co-bullying

Sadly, many coparents are coparenting with an individual whose behavior is highly defensive. This coparent may have a tendency to bully you in the conversation in order to get her way. Often, a bullying coparent will not try to understand your side of things and will quickly dismiss you or your ideas.

Other characteristics are name-calling or degrading you in front of the children and/or public, and constantly blaming you and others for the negative things she has endured. In cases of financial support, there may be attempts to withhold child support, paying it late, or not at the agreed upon times.

A bullying coparent may feel she is above the boundaries of the custody arrangement and can change plans without discussion. Likewise, she could also miss visitations without notification. Usually coparents who exhibit bullying behavior have discipline practices that can often present as yelling, humiliation, and corporal punishment. If you find that your coparent is also unreasonable and unwilling to help beyond what is required with your child, then you may have to reconsider how the relationship is impacting your child's emotional wellness and what steps you need to take to protect your child from further harm.

Children need to feel physically and emotionally safe in both parent's homes. When a child doesn't feel safe, it can be emotionally stunting, and the child will withdraw and over time manifest symptoms of anxiety and depression.

Evaluate how your child is emotionally managing his shared time with this parent. If you see signs where your child is withdrawn, agitated, anxious, or overly aggressive before and after visits, then seek professional help to have your child evaluated. You want to make sure what you are noticing about your child is not just your projection, but that an outside professional is observing the same things and may have some answers as to why. You will need to decide if the differences in one parent's home are harmful to the development of your child, then you may have to take legal action to change your custody arrangement.

THE DECISION TO LESSEN VISITS

Older children can have a preference about how much time they would like to share with their parent. It is important to discuss the reasons without judging or making them feel guilty. Be careful about having a child who doesn't feel securely attached to his parent make the decision about how much time he will spend, because he may experience an attachment wound from having to decide between parents. For younger children age thirteen and under, this is a decision that parents need to make, unless the courts have to be involved and make the decision for the family. It is a highly uncomfortable decision for grade-school children to have to decide between parents. Tweens and teens are better suited to share their preferences.

Important Points to Consider

Use the list of virtues and values in this chapter to help you decide what you have in common with your coparent, where you differ, and ideally what you want to teach in your parenting:

O Identify your top five virtues and why you value them.

O Identify your top personal challenges and how they challenge your coparenting.

O Reflect on your coparenting relationship and on which of the virtues you have most in common.

O Reflect on which virtues and values your child could currently benefit from, and how you and your coparent can support this development.

O Which of the virtues will support you in a successful coparenting relationship?

 **CHAPTER 8**

Conscious Coparenting As a United Front

Conscious coparenting requires mutual consistency for it to be at its optimum effectiveness. You want to ideally set one another up for success with your child by leveraging each other's strengths to support your child's development. To many, coparenting as a united front may seem antithetical. However, when you think about raising a child mindfully, there has to be a mutual exchange between parents about how their child will be raised. Your coparent is part of your village of support for your child.

Coparents Can Function As a Team

If you think about your coparenting relationship as a high-functioning team effort with the result being kids who are healthy, securely connected, and self-correcting, then ideally it will take both of you to make this team optimally effective. Let's take a look at five qualities that can make a huge impact on coparenting. Patrick Lencioni's book, *The Five Dysfunctions of a Team,* inspired the following qualities.

The five functioning qualities of highly effective conscious coparents are: first, trusting your coparent's ability to make decisions for your child. Second, coparents are able to handle conflict well with one another. Third, coparents are committed to being a part of their child's life. Fourth, coparents are accountable to one another for their parental commitments. Fifth, coparents pay attention to the results of their parenting efforts with one another.

Case Study: Megan and Nathan

Megan and Nathan met in college and were the best of friends. They loved their friendship so much that it seemed appropriate to marry. Once married, Megan began to realize that although she had married a dear friend, she unfortunately didn't feel passion toward him. Her discovery happened a year after getting pregnant and having a son they named Joshua. Megan and Nathan were able to process that Nathan had been feeling the same as Megan, and it was best for them to divorce, but they very much still loved each other as friends and wanted to coparent together. Megan and Nathan worked out a custody plan and were equally involved in Joshua's daily care. They continued to get along so well that they had outings together with their son, and the relationship worked. A couple of years into their divorce, Megan met Dan; she fell in love with him and married him a year later. That same year Nathan met Sandra; he fell in love with her and married her two years later. Both Megan and Nathan found partners who respected the coparenting relationship they had and wanted to be a part of Joshua's life. The four adults based their friendship on respect and care. Eventually, Megan and Dan had another son, Ethan, and they asked Nathan and Sandra to be his godparents. Nathan and Sandra felt honored to be asked to be a part of little Ethan's life because he was such an important part of Joshua's life.

Skill 1: Trust Your Coparent's Ability to Make Decisions for Your Child

Trust is the confidence in a coparent that his intentions are good. If a mistake happens in the coparent's relationship with the child, you can trust that your coparent will manage it, and it will not be used against him. The coparent is able to admit parental weaknesses and vulnerabilities and can make requests for help as needed. This secure coparent does not feel the need to protect himself and does not allow competition with his coparent to take priority over their child. The child comes first.

WHEN COPARENTS LACK TRUST IN THEIR PARENTING PARTNERSHIP

Coparents who had a previous intimate relationship may have difficulty with the concept of trusting their coparent because there is a significant emotional history between them as lovers and/or spouses, so the parenting gets muddled in this previous history. In Isolina Ricci's book *Mom's House, Dad's House*, Ricci reminds her readers to separate the past intimate relationship with more of a business relationship, and your child is the business. Conscious coparenting needs to start with an intention where you can separate your past relationship. You need to grieve the loss, reflect on the whole history, and then embark on a new role in your ex-partner's life as a coparent. Some coparents are not able to bridge this new identity in each other's life because ex-partners still want the same level of emotional access to each other. If so, then issues around trust continue.

Conscious coparents who lack trust with each other:

O Try to conceal their parenting weaknesses out of the fear of making a mistake or having ramifications with the other coparent.

O Hesitate or are resistant to ask for help from the other coparent because they assume asking for help will be held against them. This coparent may have a tendency to do things on her own and doesn't know how to ask for help when necessary.

O Resist offering help outside their shared time with their child.

- Make negative conclusions and assumptions about the intentions of their coparent based on their history together.

- Resist asking for help or collaborating with their coparent when it is in the best interests of their child.

- Hold grudges against their coparent based on their prior history.

- Avoid working together and having important conversations about their child.

Rather than avoid important topics, choose to be direct and set aside ample scheduled time to have discussions. As a result, feeling rushed will not get in the way, and conversations can be intentional.

Case Study: Ben and Judy

Ben and Judy decided to divorce after several difficult years of arguments, as well as Ben's exceptionally busy travel schedule for work. Ben and Judy had decided on an eighty-twenty custody arrangement because of Ben's rigorous work schedule, and agreed he would see the children on the weekends. Judy was flexible with the weekend arrangement because she just wanted the kids to have a relationship with their father. Even though she could no longer live with Ben, she still wanted their children to know Ben and all he had to offer as a dad.

When Ben was in town and initially came to visit the kids, he would not take the children to his place. Judy encouraged him to set up the kids' bedrooms at his house so it was comfortable for them to visit, and yet Ben continued to resist. She also noticed that Ben would drop off the kids an hour earlier than what was agreed, and the kids would sometimes not have eaten dinner. Ben wouldn't acknowledge that he was bringing the children back earlier, and after a while, the kids seemed to be a little stir-crazy after their time with Dad. After the third time of Ben bringing the kids back early, Judy asked him into the house so she could talk about his visit with the kids. Ben acknowledged that Judy had done all the work when it came to raising the kids, and he had been completely hands off. He didn't know what to do with the kids during his time, and so rather than taking the kids to the park or to the movies, he thought it best to just bring the kids back to her house. Judy, conscious of Ben's willingness to be vulnerable with her and probably feeling sensitive as well, asked Ben how she could support him having successful visits with their two children. Judy asked this not to enable Ben, but because she knew the children would benefit if their dad felt more confident in his abilities as their parent. Ben wasn't initially sure how Judy could help, so she asked him if it would be helpful to him if she put together a list of places the kids enjoy. Places where he could take them during his shared time. Ben liked the idea and asked if Judy would consider putting a set of clothes together for the kids and a list of things they would like in their rooms at his house. Ben had gotten so used to living out of his suitcase, that he honestly didn't feel comfortable trying to put together a home. Judy recognized that it was a big step for Ben to reach out for help, and she knew her kids would benefit if she helped their dad set things up for his time with them.

CONSCIOUS COPARENTS WHO WORK WELL TOGETHER

The following is a list of traits that successful conscious coparents display:

O Can admit parenting deficits, seek help to increase their abilities, and acknowledge when they have made a mistake to their child, and if necessary to their coparent

O Can ask for help from their coparent and outside support network

O Accepts parental responsibility

O Gives their coparent the benefit of the doubt before coming to a negative conclusion about their behavior

O Effectively communicates and offers feedback to their coparent with a supportive and encouraging approach

O Looks for opportunities to highlight the skillset and experiences each coparent can offer their child

- Keeps the focus when communicating solely on their child and coparenting issues

- Can offer and accept apologies between coparents about parenting issues

- Engages in parenting discussions with the coparent to ensure a timely execution of parenting responsibilities

---

A way to build more trust is to acknowledge the contributions your coparent is making in your child's life. Acknowledgments that are specific help affirm your coparent and build into the new roles you are both playing as coparents.

HOW DO YOU BUILD TRUST?

Increasing the level of trust between coparents takes time, and you need to be realistic about how much time building trust will take based on how difficult the dissolution of the intimate relationship was. Because you have positive coparenting experiences with each other, where you experience each other following through on what was agreed upon in your coparenting practices, the trust will increase. So be courteous, follow through on what you commit to, and do not overcommit; otherwise, you are setting up unrealistic expectations for your coparent, your child, and ultimately yourself. If you have a tendency to overcommit and can't deliver, look further at this pattern because it tears down trust in relationships over time.

Skill 2: Handle Conflict Well

Coparents who had conflict in their past marital relationship may continue to feel anxious about conflict in their coparenting. Some people are more conflict avoidant by nature. Many people assume that when there is conflict, there has to be a fight. Coparents who had a history of unfair fighting practices may dread having to handle problems with each other. Important topics for your child may be purposefully avoided because it is too uncomfortable for you to broach them with your coparent, and it inadvertently causes more problems for your child.

HANDLING CONFLICT WELL CALLS FOR BEING BRAVE

You are encouraged to be brave. You have a new role in your coparent's life, and you have a duty to your child to handle issues concerning your child's welfare. Avoid character assassination where you personalize the fighting with your coparent. In fact, if you and your coparent can handle conflict productively together, it will often leave both of you feeling a bit uncomfortable because you have probably both compromised on an issue.

Another helpful advantage to conflict is that it can sharpen your parenting skills if you are open to objective feedback. Coparents can solve problems if they are willing to bring up issues respectfully with each other. In addition, it models handling conflict in a healthy way to your child. This is particularly important if your child saw you frequently argue when you were together. If conflict in your coparenting is still a significant block to getting along more productively, then consider asking your coparent if going to counseling would be helpful in addressing certain issues. Attending counseling is typically for individuals who are more growth minded and see the counseling as a helpful mediation tool with their coparent. The whole purpose is to focus on your parenting partnership.

Skill 3: Commit to Both Being a Part of Your Child's Life

The investment is clear. Both parents want to be equally engaged in raising their child. When commitment to raising their child is apparent, coparents are better able to unite themselves behind decisions that are ideal for their child.

The direction and priorities for the child can be easier to see when both parents are committed, so both are able to move forward in their parenting without hesitation, and reduce their parenting guilt. Guilt reduction occurs because the decisions you are making for your child are not solely on your shoulders; you and your coparent are working on them.

When coparents fail to commit, there are struggles with being directionless and unable to hone in on your child's priorities. This ambiguity can cause unnecessary delays that can impact your child. For example, you found a preschool that you really want your child to attend but your coparent is dragging his heals and is resisting signing up, and by the time the decision is made, the preschool spot is gone.

Another consequence of lacking commitment is you start to lack confidence in your coparent's abilities and parent on your own. Some coparents want to display self-inadequacy and have the other parent make the majority of the decisions. If this is the case, then you may have to re-evaluate how much shared time your coparent can realistically handle with your child. Indecision can also cause unnecessary circular discussions because you aren't accomplishing anything.

SCHEDULE A WEEKLY MEETING WITH YOUR COPARENT

There is a business aspect to raising children well. It requires organization and consistency. Coparents who are committed to working well together for the sake of their child can benefit from scheduling a weekly call to address any concerns, upcoming schedule issues, and the child's progress at school and overall development. If you find that you really struggle relationally when working with your coparent, then use e-mail to list your bullet points. E-mails can be helpful because you will have documentation on what was covered. Consider using a list similar to this to cover the following topics:

○ **Health and wellness:** any changes or updates to your child's health. Evaluate medications, scheduling doctor's appointments, and who will be driving.

○ **Academics:** Evaluate how your child is doing in school. Which areas might your child need more help in regarding homework, and what strategies should you implement to support your child's academic success?

○ **Sports/hobbies:** Evaluate how your child is feeling about his team sport or hobby. Evaluate any logistical concerns with getting your child to and from practices, games, or classes.

○ **Social:** Evaluate how much time your child has to spend with friends outside of class and decide if there are any opportunities to have friends over, and on which coparent's time.

○ **Schedule for following week:** Update each other on your child's schedule and on any additional events, like school functions, game schedules, birthday parties, and family events.

○ **Previous business that needs addressing:** Follow up with each other on any issues previously addressed but not completed. These issues can consist of anything pertaining to your child.

○ **Any upcoming business to cover for your child:** Any upcoming changes for your child that need preparation, such as change of health insurance, transitions for parents, summer camps, vacations, and so on.

Online calendars like Google Calendar can make coordinating with your coparent much easier and more efficient. Speak at the beginning of the week about how you both will coordinate your child's schedule and then use the online calendar to set reminders and reviews with one another.

Using an agenda when meeting weekly to discuss and coordinate how your child is doing helps create structure for the meeting. Reviewing the key decisions made at each of your coparenting meetings will help reinforce what you discussed and clarify the action plan for the following week. Some parents may be resistant to a weekly coparenting meeting, but consider how your child will benefit from your organization with each other. Having a set plan helps your children feel safer and reduces anxiety. Parents will feel more organized and on task for their child, knowing what to expect of the other coparent. Children feel more secure knowing which parent will be at pickup, or which parent will help with a certain homework assignment.

NEW TRANSITIONS WITH YOUR CHILD

Speaking to your coparent about a new transition before you discuss it with your child is a good idea, so your coparent can be better prepared to help your child with the transition. For example, a parent taking a new job and deciding to move out of state is a big deal. Speaking about the ramifications of the move with your coparent helps the parent consciously prepare for the move himself, so he can better support your child's emotions about the parent moving. Using the meeting is not asking your coparent for permission. You are free to make your own decisions, but it is to best help you navigate this emotional terrain. Coparents need to talk about any issue that is going to impact their child.

Dating and spending time with the new person is a tougher topic to discuss. This is a coparenting meeting conversation topic only when your child is spending a significant amount of time with your new intimate partner, or you are transitioning the relationship to moving in together, and/or marriage. The coparenting meeting should ideally be for the two primary caregivers of the child, not stepparents or dating relationships. Stepparents are secondary caregivers, and the primary caregivers need to give directions to the stepparents.

Skill 4: Accountability

In order for coparents to work well together, accountability is a helpful tool to ensure things get done in a timely manner for your child. Accountability means tolerating the personal discomfort of calling out your coparent on behavior and not avoiding difficult conversations. This proves more difficult if you are really angry, or you don't want to hurt your coparent's feelings. Not saying something proves problematic because resentment can fester if your coparent is losing credibility with you and you do not say anything. Keeping one another accountable as coparents demonstrates that you respect your coparent, and you are committed to consciously parenting well together. When coparents lack accountability in their partnership, it is easier for parenting results to have more of an individual focus, rather than a team focus. Turning to one's own needs as a parent alienates your coparent, and potentially the true needs of your child.

Highly effective coparents who hold each other accountable can also identify potential problems quickly by questioning one another's approaches without hesitation. Problems can be identified and spoken about quickly because there is mutual respect for how you both parent and the role you each play in your child's life. The focus is on the parenting and what your child needs most. A good example of effective accountability is when one parent has had to discipline by taking away a privilege. If the misbehavior is something both parents do not support, then working together on upholding the discipline at both homes really supports the lesson they are teaching. It also demonstrates to your child that you are consistent with what you want to teach, and the child needs to take both of you seriously when it comes to misbehavior and appropriate expectations.

Giving effective feedback on how you see your coparent contributing to your child's life also strengthens accountability because you are reinforcing what your coparent is doing well; you are also reinforcing where you think he could improve. If you rely on your coparent to be responsible only to himself, this can create avoidance of the issues. It is important to give effective feedback in a respectful manner.

Case Study: Darya and Amir

Darya and Amir had been divorced for three years and had a strong coparenting relationship, even after Amir began dating again. Their two sons, ages five and seven, really enjoyed spending time with their dad and being active with him at soccer events or playing soccer in the park. When Amir became more involved with his girlfriend, Vafa, she began spending time with Amir during his shared time. This cut down on the playtime the boys were used to having with their father, and they were resentful and sad when returning to Darya's house. Darya felt conflicted about speaking to Amir about the problem because she didn't want to come across as the ex who was jealous or trying to hinder Amir's happiness. Darya honestly wished Amir happiness because she eventually wanted to feel more content in a relationship for herself. Darya decided to take the risk. At their weekly coparenting meeting, she mentioned how the boys were feeling and added that she wasn't trying to be intrusive, but she wanted him to know how much their boys loved time with their dad. Amir listened and appreciated the feedback. He followed up on his own with the boys. They admitted they wanted more time with him but didn't want to say anything because they knew their dad really liked Vafa. Amir decided to organize his shared time differently by spending three-quarters of his time with the boys and have Vafa join them occasionally. He decided to spend time with Vafa on his off time.

Skill 5: Pay Attention to Results

The end result that all parents want is to raise healthy and happy kids who are self-motivated and desire closely connected relationships. A coparenting team who focuses collaboratively on the end result will continue to grow and put what is best for the child at the forefront of the coparenting relationship. Often the end result of all the efforts is seen in glimpses during the childhood years, and then in full bloom by the college years. Plan to see the proverbial bonus in your coparenting much later.

Paying attention to the results also lets you know where your child needs more effort and attention. Rather than blaming each other and becoming defensive, choosing to mutually accept responsibility and make necessary changes will get you a quicker solution. For example, if your child brings home a report card with several Cs and two Bs, some coparents might blame one another for not helping enough with homework. But paying attention to the results means evaluating all the factors that are contributing to the grades and then collaborating on the solutions available to help your child have a stronger academic success.

Your child's success becomes something that coparents can celebrate together. Likewise, the challenges give both coparents the opportunity to be present with their child and comfort her through the resiliency building. When coparents focus on working together, they align on a common goal, which is to raise their child. This focus also helps to avoid distractions, such as unhealthy comments riddled with critical or contemptuous statements. Having a common goal directs the conversations to be solely about the kids and reduces nonessential conversations.

Important Points to Consider

When conscious coparents work together, the sense of being a part of a supportive team for the child is being encouraged. Seeing your coparenting efforts in the framework of being a part of a team can help you with the following:

O Seeing coparenting as a team effort helps to put aside your own interests and prioritizes the child's needs.

O The more trust you build in your coparenting relationship, the stronger your ability to resolve conflicts successfully.

O Use an agenda to structure the conversation and speak weekly about the week's issues for your child. More time will be necessary with more children.

O Speak with your coparent first about a new transition before you tell your child. This way your coparent has a reference point for the information and can be more understanding when your child brings it up.

 **CHAPTER 9**

Rhythm and Routine

Coparents who can align on implementing a more solid rhythm during their shared time help their children internalize healthy routines. Part of the benefits of living on your own and having shared custody is the opportunity to independently develop your own routines and rhythm for your household. It may be vastly different from what you once had when you were raising your child under the same roof. For some parents, this can feel liberating, and for others, anxiety provoking. This chapter will discuss what you need to consider when deciding what kind of rhythm and routine you want to create.

What Is Rhythm and Routine?

Rhythm is the feeling or tempo of your home when you parent. As parent educator and marriage and family therapist Nola Casserly states about rhythm, "Following a rhythm is more like a dance where you live, moving according to the beats. On the other hand, *routine* is more like a checklist that stays the same every day. Rhythm can allow spontaneity to bubble up and change everything that was originally planned for the day—for example, a storm or a unique opportunity that presents itself suddenly. Rhythm is flexible yet foundational." How do you want *your home* to feel to your child?

Children who are stimulus seeking and sensory driven gravitate toward more stimulation. These children have heightened regulatory systems that have a hard time calming down. A useful tool to help children calm down is to fill a bin or deep tray with dried lentils or beans. Have your child immerse his arms in the tray. The coolness and smoothness of the beans provides a sensory stimulation, and it elicits a calming sensation. Another calming tool is a warm bath. If you have a child with sensory deficits and would like to understand this further, consider reading *The Out-of-Sync Child* by Carol Stock Kranowitz.

The day's rhythm consists of breathing-in moments and breathing-out moments. *Active breathing-out* moments are points of the day where stimulation and activity are occurring. *Reflective breathing in* means being present with an activity with your child and coming back to connect with oneself. Both are important, and your day should have varied moments of each. Too much active breathing out can become too chaotic and anxiety provoking. Too little can be boring and unstimulating. Striking the balance between these moments sets the rhythm of your life. Shared time with your child may have a different rhythm than when your child is with his other parent. Rhythm can be adaptable, and the more regulated you are emotionally, the more flexibility you may have with your rhythm.

ACTIVE BREATHING MOMENTS

Children need adequate stimulation and activity for healthy development. Adding breathing-out moments to the rhythm of your child's day offers points of stimulation and expansion for the child to engage with his world. For some children, the need for a lot of activity and movement is important. For example, anyone who is raising boys understands the utter necessity for wrestling time. These natural expressions manifest in environments that allow boys to imagine and move. Active breathing during the day also consists of going to class and being alert and engaged with the academic environment.

REFLECTIVE BREATHING MOMENTS

Reflective breathing represents quiet inward movement. Finding key points in the day to slow down or take in and reflect helps the child stay grounded and restored after activity. There are certain points in the day when school-age children need reflective breathing moments. A breathing-in moment consists of children feeling their parent's presence with them. As Helle Heckmann wrote in the article "Daily Rhythm at Home and Its Lifelong Relevance," "You have to try to find out when the children breathe in and when they breathe out. And when the children are in the breathing-in period, you have to make sure you are present, so the child feels *ah, here I feel my parents, and they are there for me.*"

Conscious coparents who provide a sense of being there for their children are teaching them to breathe in deeply and soak in the sense of feeling felt and seen. When you first see your child when waking him up, picking him up from school, or picking him up for your shared time, make sure to be as present as you can be by greeting him with open arms, maintaining eye contact, and taking in his presence. Your child will experience that you are with him and breathing in during your shared time together. Coparents who pick up their child on their initial arrival and are on the phone, completing a text, talking with other parents, or bring friends or new relationships to their initial transition will miss out on that first breathing-in moment with their child. Emergencies happen, and work does sometime call you after hours, but give yourself and your child that initial moment to greet one another with full presence. You can explain you need a little time after to complete your work. More than likely, if you have been fully present with your child upon the initial greeting, he will be gracious about the time.

There are particular points of the day when being fully present for your child ignites breathing in, and sets the day's rhythm in motion. The first is upon waking up and starting the day. Embracing the quiet and emerging hustle and bustle start of the day is easier when a child has enough time to wake up, take care of hygiene, make his bed, and have a healthy breakfast. The morning time should not feel rushed. As David Elkind wrote in his classic book *The Hurried Child*, "Rushing is toxic."

Rushing truly is toxic for children. Rushing often is at the center of many parental/child misbehavior issues.

The toxic rushing cycle goes like this: the parent needs the child to hurry so the parent or child won't be late, which leads to the child feeling anxious, which leads to the parent feeling more anxious, which leads to escalation, and the process being slowed up even more. Morning time needs to be protected with ample time and preparation on the parent's part. Waking up early and taking care of your own agenda before you get the kids up can help tremendously with this.

Taking a little downtime after school for children to have free play is another key moment in the day to breathe out. Many children are so used to being entertained through screens that they are skipping foundational ages to free play. Play has been shown to increase intelligence, creativity, and foster imagination. Play is also a key way for children to relieve stress. Organized sports and structured exercise provide lessons in teamwork, discipline, performance, as well as learning to master a skill. But keep in mind that sports can also be stressful as the level of competition increases. Free play provides a stress-free experience where whatever the child imagines is good enough. Children receive so many messages that question their "being enough"; it is such a gift to give them the space to just be without comparisons for a little bit of each day.

Understand "the gift of boredom" for your child. Boredom can actually be the catalyst for creative thought and expression. If you challenge your child to be bored, have him come up with a list of different things he can do that is not TV or video game related. Have arts and craft supplies on hand that encourage creativity. Ask your child what supplies he may need if he comes up with an idea. A little boredom can go a long way!

Another area where breathing in is supported is in the family rhythm once dinner is complete. Set routines that let your child know it's time to prepare for the night. Quiet activities, such as a regular bath time, story reading, dimming the lights, or lighting a candle are cues that the evening is here and it is time to wind down. It's a routine signal that bedtime is near, and your body needs to begin to prepare for the end of the day. Setting up cues for your child that tells her the rhythm of the home is changing back to one of quiet helps parents who may have difficulty with rowdy children before bed. Once you create a regular routine of cues, your child will become familiar with them and internalize the rhythm.

CREATING BREATHING-IN AND BREATHING-OUT MOMENTS

Conscious coparents are mindful of how their child's day breathes. You want the rhythm of your home to reflect your personality, but not to the extent where it deprives your child of a healthy rhythm and compromises her development. For example, some people can visit three friends for breakfast, then meet someone for lunch, attend a birthday party in the afternoon, head off to dinner and a movie, and then fall into bed by 10 P.M. each night. If you have an "I can fit it all in attitude" to take on this kind of jam-packed day frequently, then you may not be considering how your child's day breathes. Take into account your child's temperament and the kind of stimulation and downtime she requires. Your children can stretch their internal rhythm on occasions, but too much stretching over continuous days may cause additional misbehavior because they are tired and have sensory overload. A conscious coparent, when given the information ahead of time of what their child may be doing with their coparent, may be selective about scheduling too much the day before. Being mindful of your child having downtime so he has energy to take in a special activity, like an amusement park, is extremely important for his well-being. Discuss with your coparent if you intend to take your child to a fun activity so you don't overbook or repeat the same outings. Maintaining a child's sense of wonder is protected when you don't overschedule or have too many entertaining engagements in succession.

VACATIONS AND RHYTHMS

Scheduling vacations for conscious coparents is also an opportunity to be mindful of rhythm. Scheduling vacations at different times whenever possible, and not close together, helps the child to be more present on the vacation with each coparent and helps her take in the wholeness of the experience. Scheduling summer vacation might look like one vacation in June, while the other coparent's vacation is in July. Vacations that embrace a rhythm that has spontaneity, but also a few similar points to the home rhythm, can be helpful for children who love being at home. A nightlight from home, lovey, blanket, pillow, and snacks your child typically enjoys all help ground your child when staying in a new place.

Vacations that include activity and downtime each day are ideal for children. You might be tempted to compare vacations your coparent is taking with the kids or get angry if you had wanted to take your kids on the same vacation. That can be disappointing, but remember that the purpose of a vacation is to have concentrated time together that you can enjoy with one another. Ask yourself, in what kind of environment are you most relaxed and present with your child outside of your home? Once you figure out your answer, look for places that will provide that experience that optimally fits into your budget.

The Value of Setting a Healthy Rhythm for Coparents

Setting a healthy rhythm to your home life for coparenting encourages your children to feel more secure and embrace the tempo of your home. Choosing a rhythm for your home has to be based on a few things: predictability, the developmental stage of your child, and your natural rhythm.

Rhythm has predictability blended into the family's tempo. Predictability builds safety and security for children. Children of divorce need predictability in both households to help them foster the sense of security that both parents are continuing to parent with their child in mind. An illustration of predictability that coparents can work on together is creating a culture of politeness in both homes. As author Kim John Payne wrote in his book *Simplicity Parenting*, "One of the simplest, purest forms of stability or predictability in daily life is politeness. It is a level of communication and interaction that can be counted on, that builds trust." This is about respecting one another and creating safety in how you approach one another in your home, as well as in the home of your coparent.

The age and developmental stage of your child is another factor that affects the rhythm of your household. Children need a tighter rhythm to their day, starting from when they are little, so they can develop and expand their self-regulation skills. A baby's natural rhythm often consists of waking and alert, eating, sleeping, wake and alert, eating, sleeping, wake and alert, eating, sleeping for a longer period, and then starting the day all over. As children grow, their developmental capacity for stimulation increases. Some children need more stimulation by way of lots of exercise because their inner rhythm needs the outlet. While other children love puttering around the house and playing inside with their toys or reading. As a coparent, you need to take into account what your child's natural rhythm is when considering the ideal rhythm for the home when you have time with your child. It is common that some children need some transition time when moving from house to house. This is particularly common with custody arrangements where you see your child every other week, or for an extended period in the summer. The younger the child, the slower the rhythm of your home typically needs to flow, so your child can continue to grow up with consistency and security. As child development expert Ronald Morrish once stated, "Start small, stay close, insist, follow through."

Your own temperament and natural rhythm need to be considered when figuring out how you want your home to flow. You may have the kind of temperament that enjoys quiet, and raising children may challenge how much quiet you are able to embrace. Or you might relate more to enjoying a chaotic household with frequent visitors, playdates, and things to do. Think about the pace of your job and lifestyle when you are with your children and not with your children. You may be used to a faster pace of life because that is just what you are used to. Is what you are used to actually what your natural rhythm is? Consider what you want your home life to feel like. If you have a job that is stressful and/or demanding, then you might consider that your home life should have a quieter more restful flow. Working against your natural rhythm during the week can lead to chronic stress.

What was the rhythm and routine of your home growing up? Are there similarities or differences to how you are living now? What do you prefer?

WHEN RHYTHM GETS SIDETRACKED

There are occasions and seasons when the rhythm of your household goes haywire. The causes vary, but they can range from illness, divorcing, moving, adding more to the schedule, sport seasons, job transitions, financial issues, or even the loss of a loved one. When you first begin coparenting, this season has the potential to be a highly stressful time because emotionally you are feeling the pressure to manage things perfectly so your child doesn't undergo more stress or worry than necessary. Families sustain seasons when things are more chaotic or stressful for only short amounts of time. This is because the family's ability to manage stress depends on how the family has managed stress in the past, and how extensive the previous stressor was. Think of the ability to handle stress in terms of bandwidth. Some families with a greater bandwidth have dealt with past stressors, like the loss of a loved one or managing a chronic illness of a parent, and can cope with the issues more effectively. The bandwidth is a muscle that strengthens based on how stressful issues have been dealt with in the past. Then there are other family systems where their coping mechanisms are still working on "dial-up" when handling stress. It may be that the family has not undergone much stress, or they have undergone so much chronic stress that they never got the chance to strengthen and process what had just happened because the next stressor came so quickly.

WHAT'S YOUR THRESHOLD AS A COPARENT?

When you are new to coparenting, your threshold for stress may be very limited because you are coming out of a relationship that you realized was not going to be healthy for you. You may also have certain expectations for yourself about how you *should* be managing your new life as a coparent. Looking at what you can manage stress-wise is important to your own self-care and ability to be present with your children. If you are chronically managing chaotic schedules, it is essential that you then "prune back" so you can return to a rhythm that is more sustainable for the overall well-being of your household.

The Value of Setting a Healthy Routine for Coparents

Routines help families retain anchoring moments to the daily life of the family system. Having regular chore days, homework times, mealtimes, and bedtimes all help a child feel more secure about the family's routine. Coparents who can find common ground on the basics for their child help reinforce healthy habits but also maintain consistency in both homes.

Children thrive on consistency, and routine helps them internalize the schedule of the family. Coparents can work together to create a consistent routine that benefits their child.

Routines can focus on a certain meal for a day of the week, a schedule for chores, and a regular event for that day. Even with your child living in two different homes, it is possible to have regular routines. If you have 50–80 percent shared time, there are definitely responsibilities your child can have in your household, provided they are age appropriate. You might have to adapt the routines so they are conducive to the shared time schedule. For example, if you have a one week on and one week off schedule, regular routines are possible to implement every week your child is back at your home. Routines will vary depending on the household, and working with your coparent on similar routines will most likely not be a fruitful conversation because your coparent may want to have her own routines. The conversation that is better suited for coparenting is what are the routines your child thrives on?

SLEEP ROUTINES

Coparents who can generally align on the same bedtime hour for their child help reinforce healthy sleep habits. When a child is able to go to sleep at the same time in both homes, her biological clock can remain set. If the sleep time is vastly different in both homes, then the child can have difficulty with being overtired and catching a second wind, which disrupts the sleep cycle and the child's alertness the following day. Conscious coparents are mindful of the sleep needs of their child. If you have a child age five or younger who still benefits from napping and her nap does not affect her nighttime sleep, then you have to incorporate her nap schedule into your shared time.

Children sleeping at different homes can sometimes cause sleep issues because they may be adjusting to sleeping in a different space. Do your best to be present with your child's sleep concerns to create as much comfort as possible for her. For example, if your child is scared of the dark at your home, find out as much information as you can about what makes your child's room scary to her. Hear what your child may need in order to adjust. It may take a couple of weeks, but it should subside if you attune well and check in about how your child is feeling with the changes. Ask your coparent if he notices any sleep issues so you can potentially problem solve together. Bedtime routines are ideal to keep intact after a divorce or separation because they are routines your child is already familiar with and doesn't have to give up after a family system has changed.

NUTRITION

Nutrition is another routine area that you can create with your coparent. Considering the nutritional needs of your child at mealtimes, and providing healthy meals low in sugar, help your child develop healthy eating habits and an early association to a healthy lifestyle. You can't control what your coparent chooses to serve for dinner. However, conscious coparents should consider what their child will eat when making dinner plans. For example, it is not fair to expect a five-year-old to sit down patiently at a five-star restaurant for a three-hour meal. Set your child up for success and keep dinner routines that are doable for your child.

Although you may enjoy trying new things, children are often creatures of habit. Don't make food a battle in your home. If you leave healthy foods available and model eating well, your child will most likely adapt at some point. If you have a child who doesn't like to eat vegetables, look into vegetarian protein powders as a sneaky way to add in the nutrients he needs.

Creating New Rituals in Your Home

Children will often want to maintain rituals that were important to them growing up in their former households. A conversation with your child about what holiday rituals he liked best is a good idea because you are sharing power with your child about how you both want to enjoy the holiday. Take into account the memories your child has around certain holidays that are positive. You may want to create your own rituals in your home with your child. Invite your child into the process and see what you create together. This way the new ritual becomes something that you both have an appreciation for. If you find that your past experiences did not have enough ritual, now is the opportunity to create something new and long-standing for your family. Some examples of rituals around holiday time may be:

○ Opening one present on Christmas Eve

○ A special meal that happens on the holiday

○ Engaging each other on what each of you is thankful for

○ Special books that you read only during the holiday season

○ Special annual outings

○ A visit to see relatives during the holiday

These rituals help children feel more connected to the holidays and will help you create some holiday routines that you can look forward to in your own home. You may encounter initial sadness that your rituals and routines are without the other coparent. This varies based on your relationship with your coparent. If you have a working friendship that enables you to put your child first, then it might be possible to share holidays together. If you have a coparenting relationship where it is better to keep things more separate, then make the conscious choice to accept the boundaries needed. In the long run, you are supporting your child in having healthier holidays with one of you rather than two of you present but not getting along.

A family dinner, or a simple family breakfast that is a regular routine, builds in quality time for a family. Learn some creative conversation games to play at the table so the family can practice having one unified conversation, like "roses and thorns" or "what was the highlight and the low light of your day?" Through this regular time, your child can practice etiquette and social skills, as well as connect with you.

SIMPLIFYING SCHEDULES

Simplifying your schedule during your time with your child will help you spend more quality time together. Overscheduled families spend less concentrated time together. In these households, there is often a rushed feeling of having to rush off to the next practice, class, and so on. As a result of being overscheduled, children miss out on deepening their concentration levels. We live in a world that totes the value of multitasking, and yet the research is showing that innovation is decreasing because society is losing the ability to deeply concentrate. In addition, a child's busy schedule creates an expectation of being constantly entertained. Simply put, there is great value to "downtime." It recharges the body, mind, and the spirit. If you have a coparenting schedule where you do not see your child for a few days, taking the first hour to just spend time together and not being over-scheduled will help your child readjust to his time with you. You want your time to be meaningful, so make space for time together.

Overscheduling can also cause behavioral issues that are simply the result of your child being tired and overwhelmed. When you consider your shared time with your child, notice if he is overscheduled and how the family is doing with the schedule. Add realistic margins to drop-off and pickup, so you are not stressing yourself or your child more than necessary.

Try the "silent bite." Depending on the age of your children, add a brief pause before eating to practice the discipline of making space for intentional eating. This practice is an expression of gratitude for the food before you, and it slows down your eating process so you take in what you are about to eat. It is also a reminder that many children in the world go hungry, and you are thankful for the food before you. The silent bite, of course, depends on your child's age and capability.

WHAT DO YOU WANT THE QUALITY OF YOUR TIME TO EMBODY?

Quality time is actually the combination of both quality *and* how much time you are spending with your child. When you reflect on the rhythm of your household, making sure you have connective time with your child is a must. The quality of the time needs to be relational where you and your child are feeling connected in being together. For many families, other items like TV, video games, music, and the Internet can become substitutes for a relationship. There are thousands of American families with TVs in every room, so everyone can watch their own show and avoid fighting each other for control of the TV. The downside to this is that families become more isolated and less relational, even around family entertainment.

What is the rhythm of your household? Consider what you need to implement for improvement. How would you implement this action step?

Some families also emphasize how much money they spend on a gift or experience to equate how much they love someone. In coparenting households, this can sometimes happen when a coparent feels guilty about not being as available, so she spends money to replace the lost time and connection. Things can never replace a connective relationship. When a person feels truly connected to another and has the experience of being seen and heard, it is irreplaceable. If you find yourself substituting things for your time, then acknowledge it and make the necessary changes. When you have time with your child, focus on the relationship.

Choosing a few activities with your kids where spending money is not a part of spending time together is a helpful tool because you have a go-to list if you are wondering what to do next. Consider the following:

O Going on a nature walk

O Athletic activities

O Playing together in the park

- Regular library day
- Volunteering together
- Seeking out fun experiences, like geocaching
- Visiting museums
- Crafting

Important Points to Consider

Having a rhythm and routine that fits your individuality but also accounts for the developmental stage of your child, and your child's current needs, are major factors in creating the ideal home life you want to provide. Here are some thoughts when figuring out what your ideal rhythm at home is:

- Rhythm has predictability blended into the family's tempo. Predictability builds the safety and security children need in co-parenting households. Children like knowing what to expect next.

- When thinking about your ideal rhythm, ask yourself what you want your children to feel when they are home with you.

- When you first see your child when waking him up, picking him up from school, or picking him up for your shared time, make sure to be as present as you can be by greeting him with open arms and maintaining eye contact.

- If you are chronically managing chaotic schedules with your co-parent, do your best to cut back so you can return to a rhythm that is more sustainable for the overall well-being of your household.

- A child who is used to a busy schedule creates the expectation of having to be constantly entertained.

- Children need plenty of open-ended time that will naturally grow their imaginations. They just need the *space* to do it.

**CHAPTER 10**

Mutual Respect in Conscious Coparenting

In every coparenting relationship, there are going to be moments where you disagree and have to find a way to resolve the conflict. Conflict has an unsettling feeling for many people, and particularly for those who are conflict avoidant. Coparents who struggle with avoiding conflict tend to have difficulty with people being angry with them. They may also lack assertiveness skills and consequently have a hard time asking for what they want. Another concern is being scared to rock the boat with your coparent because there is previous history of not being able to work through the conflict. As a result, using the kids passive-aggressively to get back at your ex is common for coparents who are challenged by conflict and fear revenge or some kind of backlash.

Communication Skills

Concerns over conflict are valid if you have had previous experiences with a coparent who does not fight fair. In fact, it is these experiences that color your ability to speak up in future circumstances. Rather than letting your past dictate the outcomes of future dialogues with your coparent, let's take some time to reflect on healthy ways to communicate your needs as a coparent. Getting clear on what you need to speak about with your coparent helps to identify issues that you should address, versus issues that could work themselves out.

Parenting falls into two categories: protecting and promoting your children. You must bring it to the attention of your coparent if there are areas where your child may be at risk or needs resources to be healthy and whole.

Refraining from conversations with your coparent that come across as judgmental or nitpicky about your coparent's skills or choices helps to foster a friendlier working relationship. If you try to control how your coparent behaves, this will corrupt your coparent's ability to discuss problems with you, and create more of a parallel parenting dynamic. Be selective about intervening, and do so when it is important to the raising and care of your child. This way your words will have more credibility and others will view your assertions with more seriousness than an overreaction.

Several conflict management skills may be helpful. Let's look at a few tools that may be helpful to use when working with your coparent:

DISARMING TECHNIQUE

Used in cognitive behavioral therapy by Dr. David Burns, the disarming technique is an initial statement in an antagonistic conversation where the individual who is being adversely addressed finds some kind of genuine truth that he can agree with in the argument. The result is the person who was bringing up the issue feels caught off guard because you see his point. For example, your coparent brings up that you were late picking up the kids the last two times, and it causes problems for him to get to work on time. You would genuinely reply, "You're right. I have been late the last couple of times, and I can see it has put you in a bind."

Finding something you can somewhat agree on is all that is needed. It doesn't mean you have to agree entirely with what the person is saying. For example, your coparent says to you, "You really need to make more of an effort to attend Jake's basketball games. He feels completely unloved by you and this isn't the first time he has felt that way." On the outside, this has the potential to be a hurtful statement if you take it personally. In addition, it is said with the hope that it will be taken personally because your coparent wants you to feel bad. To disarm might sound like "Jake's basketball games are really important to him, and I am glad you brought up that attending the games make him feel loved. Note taken." Acknowledging what is true can help diffuse uncomfortable conversations and accusations. If the coparent reacted poorly to this accusation, then you would get embroiled in the argument instead of hearing Jake's truth of wanting his parents to attend his basketball games.

AVOID DISTRACTION STATEMENTS

Distraction statements are statements that take the conversation off task. People often distract as a way to manipulate or reduce anxiety. It can also be a defensive mechanism because you do not want to address a difficult subject. Distraction statements may also cause arguments in another topic, which is actually in the coparent's mind. For example, your coparent says, "Stacy needs to be in this dance class that's four days a week and costs $300 more per month. I would like to split the costs; however, you should really be paying for all of it because you make more money than I do. I really pay for more than I should." Do your best to ignore the rabbit hole in the conversation, and address the actual issue, saying something to the effect of, "Stacy is a wonderful dancer, and I am glad she loves her classes. I am happy to pay for half the class and will send my $150 to the dance school today." Distraction statements have the capacity to dig up old hurts, and you can avoid the landmines by ignoring them and sticking to the facts in the conversation.

EVALUATING IF IT'S YOUR NEED OR YOUR CHILD'S

Reflecting on the purpose of your request is important to consider before you speak with your coparent. Ask yourself the following question: Is this request for me or for my child?

Say the request you have is your child has wanted to have a sleepover with her new best friend from school, and the date the friend's mom offered fell on your coparent's weekend. You could share the information of the invitation and the reasons why you think it would be a good idea for your daughter to attend the sleepover. Ultimately, because it is your coparent's weekend, he would have the right to refuse. This kind of request is one that benefits your child. It would be up to the coparent who will miss the time to evaluate if he is willing to forgo the time. A request that benefits you, such as asking to switch weekends to accommodate a getaway with your friends, is a different matter. Evaluating how often you have asked to switch weekends may be part of this discussion, as it may be difficult for your coparent to change his calendar when he relies on the schedule to make plans.

Under no circumstances should you use your child as a pawn to get back at your coparent for something you feel resentful about. Children can feel the tension between their parents, and they ultimately pay the cost with this kind of behavior.

If the request is a benefit to you, then you need to ask yourself a follow-up question: If this request is for me, what am I able to negotiate with my coparent? Using the previous example, you might ask to switch weeks or look to forgo a makeup for your weekend altogether. What you try to negotiate also depends on the personality of your coparent. If you are collaborating with a coparent who really enjoys his family life, this request may not be an issue. In fact, some coparents write in a first right of refusal to be able to have the kids rather than use a daycare provider during the other coparent's shared time if trips or aftercare are potentially necessary. If you are dealing with a coparent who might enjoy making matters worse between the two of you when making a request, then a better option may be looking at other daycare options if you decide to go away on a weekend when you have the kids. The ideal option would be choosing a weekend when your coparent has the kids, but you can't always count on the ideal. This is when being selective in your requests is helpful.

If you are the type of coparent who asks to change the schedule frequently, then consider how it impacts your coparent's planning. When you make repetitive schedule switches or changes, it can affect the coparenting partnership because your schedule changes can present you as not being reliable to your coparent or to your child. You also lose credibility about your desire to spend time with the kids because if you are not able to make the agreed-upon times, then that can cause your children to feel upset and potentially think that they are not important to you. It also presents as though you are not committed or compliant to the boundaries of what you initially agreed to with your coparent. Frequent schedule changes cause coparents to feel like their lives and plans don't matter, and that you consider your schedule more of a priority than spending time with your kids. Be conscious of your requests and consider how frequently you ask for schedule changes to accommodate events or work requirements. Be forthcoming with your coparent and provide plenty of notice if your work is moving into a season where you will be traveling more and perhaps need to change the schedule. Communicating about the changes of your schedule is key, and coming up with a plan to let your coparent and your children know about the changes is important. This way your children won't be taken by surprise if you cannot make it on time for pickup or if changes to the schedule occur.

THE CONSCIOUS COPARENTING APPROACH TO REQUEST MAKING

A conscious coparent takes into account how precious family time is and respects that her coparent also has a life outside of the kids. It's not your business to know about that life unless it encroaches into the children's lives. This includes job changes, living arrangement changes, other people moving into the home, remarriage, significant others who are spending more time with your child, and deaths of significant relatives for the child. If you have a request that you would like to approach your coparent with and have identified that it is a request for you, consider approaching her in the following way:

○ **Start with an appreciation:** Say something you sincerely appreciate about your coparent. Appreciations that are specific and genuine are great icebreakers and can diffuse the potential discomfort you and your coparent may have when speaking with each other. A statement such as, "Hi, Laura, I want you to know how much I appreciate your ability to sit with our kids and help them with homework. Your patience is really paying off, and they are doing so well in school as a result. Thank you for your diligence."

○ **Share the new change:** Give the facts of the situation that are changing for you. "I wanted to let you know ahead of time that I am having some work changes over the next month that will require me to travel during the workweek."

○ **Make the request:** "Would it be possible to change our coparenting schedule this month for different weeks with the kids? Take a look at my work changes and see if you are able to accommodate any of the changes. If not, I am also open to other solutions that you may have in mind."

Managing Resentments with Your Coparent

You do not need to share the complex intricacies of why you needed to separate or divorce with your children. Those reasons are yours and yours alone. Since you are reading a book on conscious coparenting, you more than likely gave your relationship or marriage extensive thought before changing your family's life arrangements. In order to have a workable relationship with your coparent, you have to look inward and choose to heal any resentments you may have from your prior relationship. Coming through a divorce or separation may have been one of the most painful experiences you have encountered. This pain intensifies for many parents going through divorce when they think their children did not ask for this. Finding personal meaning about the relationship will help you grow from what you experienced and move on. You may have endured a level of pain that you didn't think possible and feel bitter about the experience.

A classic story of finding meaning despite intolerable circumstances is Viktor Frankl's autobiography *Man's Search for Meaning*. Frankl shares his story of being placed into Auschwitz, a World War II concentration camp, for four years. Amid all the horror and tragedy that he witnessed and experienced on a daily basis, he recognized the one thing that the Nazi soldiers could not take away from him was his spirit and ability to find purpose. He wrote, "For the first time in my life I saw the truth as it is set into song by so many poets, proclaimed as the final wisdom by so many thinkers. The truth—that love is the ultimate and the highest goal to which man can aspire. Then I grasped the meaning of the greatest secret that human poetry and human thought and belief have to impart: The salvation of man is through love and in love."

Upon this epiphany, he extended kindness to the soldiers and was polite to them. He recognized firsthand that when he was polite and kindhearted, it shifted how the soldiers related to him. Perhaps Frankl's kindness reminded the soldiers he was still a human being—a vast difference in perspective from how the persecuted in Auschwitz were being treated. Frankl's story is one of resilience, perseverance, and love. Choosing to live from a place of love within himself changed how he was able to cope with genocide in Auschwitz. You may be coming out of your own personal hell and are living to tell the tale. Remember, you are in charge of your feelings. When you hold onto bitterness and resentment, at the end of the day it impacts you more than anyone else.

Ask yourself why you need to hold onto the bitterness. What are you getting out of holding onto past history that is triggering and hurtful to you?

The risk that is taken by surrendering to love rather than fear is trusting that the leap will be worth it. In each of our lives, we have only about

10 percent control over our circumstances, and the rest is out of our control. We would like to think we have a lot more control than this and find different ways to try to fool ourselves, but to no avail. What you do have control over is how you relate to your life, and the ability to discern what you do have control over and what you don't. Choosing to love well eradicates the fear in choice because you make decisions from a standpoint of love and its abundance, rather than fear and its depravity. A biblical quote succinctly illustrates this thought: *Perfect Love drives out all fear.* Where love abides, fear cannot take hold.

How do you love someone who you despise? By focusing on the greater goal. Love is an action as well as a feeling. If you focus on love being an action, and you love your children from both a feeling and action oriented place, then a byproduct of loving your children is to respect your working relationship with your coparent. Your coparent is a very important person in your child's life. You may not agree on everything, and you don't have to. This is why you are no longer together. However, what you both have in common is your children. Choosing to respect your coparent because you love your kids is an amazing act of love.

STAYING POSITIVE

Researcher and author Barbara Fredrickson began studying positive emotions in 1998 and developed a theory about positive emotions called the Broaden-and-Build Theory. This theory hypothesizes that positive emotions like love, joy, and gratitude play an essential role in human survival, helping humans create social and connective bonds with one another. Fredrickson's research also revealed that when people have positive emotions, they create neural pathways that are open and available to new possibilities and ideas. These positive emotions help build personal resiliency and well-being as demonstrated by the individual's physical, intellectual, and social resources. The theory also states that negative emotions like anxiety, fear, and anger work against the individual, causing the mind to hyperfocus on the real or imagined threat, which then limits one's ability to be open to new possibilities and ideas and build those inner resources used for personal development and relationships.

Fredrickson's research has some applications to coparenting. If you focus on the positive emotions you want to be present within your life and focus your attention on the positive attributes of your coparent, you will end up fostering coparenting resources that benefit your parenting partnership and the relationship with your child. If you place your focus on the negative feelings, you will only increase the level of negativity you have with your coparent. Positive emotions also help you survive as a coparent. Working together with a positive attitude will benefit everyone in your family. The new possibilities and ideas that you both can come up with together for your child may help build your child's knowledge of being loved and accepted, as well as build his inner resilience.

Researcher and author Barbara Fredrickson proved that positivity actually enhances health and wellness. Check out *www.happify.com* to learn skills to build your brain to become more productive and to build skills for lasting happiness.

You should also strive to stay positive about your coparent in front of your children. Children want to know that their parents like each other enough and can get along. It helps children feel safer and more secure with both of their caregivers. Parents who speak unkindly about their coparent, whether through direct statements or indirect statements and nonverbal gestures, give negative messages that are confusing and hurtful to their children. These types of inadvertent negative messages can be construed as the parent pushing an emotional agenda with the kids. Sadly, there are coparenting situations where children feel like one parent is pushing them to choose between their parents. This is incredibly unfair, and it stems from unprocessed residual hurt from the parent. More than likely, a history of unresolved relational trauma is causing this manipulative behavior as payback against the other coparent, but the children are hurt more.

RESPECT STARTS WITH RESPECTING YOURSELF

Feeling disrespected is a common feeling for many coparents who were initially in a relationship together. Feeling disrespected may continue, even if you are no longer in an intimate relationship, because it manifests in the coparenting. Common behaviors where people feel disrespected are chronic lateness, name-calling, feeling financially bullied, poor boundaries, not following through on commitments, and being talked down to. If you find yourself relating to any of the behaviors, or have more to add, then consider what you can do to empower yourself so you can stop feeling disrespected.

> If you find yourself in relationships where others routinely disrespect you, ask yourself where else in your life have you felt disrespected.

Typically, people who feel disrespected in their adult relationships have experienced similar feelings in past relationships. The root of feeling disrespected may stem from experiencing a loss of power or control early on. These earlier childhood memories are often traumatic and you need to process them with a mental health provider. It is vital to your present and future relationships that you work through relational trauma because any kind of trauma restricts your potential. Healing trauma offers entrance to a new way of being that cannot be taken away from you.

RESENTFUL FEELINGS AND UNMET NEEDS

Feelings of resentment are often connected to some unmet need. Identifying the need that is going unmet is the first step in effectively taking emotional care of yourself with your coparent. Needs are personal, and they are connected to thoughts of how you want to view yourself, as well as your need for respect. Consider what needs you are looking for your coparent to meet. Particular needs, such as acceptance, love, approval, and recognition may be difficult to experience in an adversarial coparenting relationship. These needs are valid, but it is wise to redirect your urge for your coparent to make you feel good about yourself. Having a community that supports you emotionally by seeing and appreciating you is important. Understanding how your unmet needs relate to your feelings toward your coparent can be a helpful compass to identifying the needs. You can also look to healthier ways, including personal relationships, to get them met.

As a conscious coparent, processing your residual issues with your coparent is key to having an effective working partnership. Being able to make sense of how you were hurt and the origins of this hurt are important for you personally, for your relationship with your kids, and for your future relationships. The outcome of choosing inner healing is the ability to feel more confident in who you are and allow you to build an inner resiliency, which will help you manage your emotions and be less reactive in potentially reactive situations with your coparent. More than likely, you will need to see a therapist you feel safe and comfortable with to really process your feelings. Friendships are amazing adjunct support with life stressors, but friendships cannot always provide concentrated time and tools to focus solely on your relational healing and the negative thoughts that you have developed about yourself as a result.

Case Study: Tara and Dean

Tara had raised two girls with Dean until their oldest, Joanna, was seven and Deanna was five. Tara knew she wanted a decent working relationship with Dean, particularly because their girls were little and needed their dad in their lives. The first couple of years after the divorce Dean and Tara were able to work well together. Dean would have the girls one day during the week and every other weekend. Then Dean met someone and decided to remarry, and Tara met someone shortly thereafter. The girls began feeling uncomfortable at Dean's house, and their stepmother was unable to foster a connection with them. The girls would come home to Tara sad. They no longer wanted to visit their dad after several occasions where their stepmom reinforced that they were not wanted or important to their new family. Tara, feeling upset for the girls, had a difficult time of communicating to Dean how the girls were feeling. Dean would feel defensive and blame Tara for poisoning the girls against his new wife. Tara had to consciously choose to listen to her girls' feelings but not speak poorly about Dean. She had been in therapy and took the time to process her anger, so the girls did not have to emotionally take on any of her burdens. She recognized it was hard enough for them to feel unimportant to their father. Tara still hoped for the girls to have a thriving relationship with their dad, but she could not control how he was behaving toward them. She redirected her girls to go to their father together and share how they felt and ask what they needed from him. The girls wanted to have alone time with their dad and no longer go to his home for overnights. Tara was conscious of not having a personal agenda for the girls. She was very clear that her intention was to help her girls develop their communication skills and have the ability to express their needs. As a result, the girls were able to speak to their father together, and a compromise was made of having their weeknight dinner be a night out with just Dean and the girls. At Dean's new home, the girls had smaller amounts of time to adjust to their new stepmom.

Skills That Foster Mutual Respect

If your goal is to have a cohesive working relationship that commands respect from one another, there are tools you can use to help build your coparenting relationship. These skills can be used in regular exchanges with each other, and they are used often in highly effective relationships.

MUTUAL RESPECT FOR SHARED CUSTODY TIME

Part of showing mutual respect for your coparent is also respecting her alone time with your children. Conscious coparenting assumes that relationships with both parents are fundamental to the child's growing sense of self. Respecting you coparent's time with your child benefits not only your coparenting relationship, but your child's developmental needs as well. Trust that your coparent is doing her best and attempting to bond well.

You might feel jealous that you have to share time with your coparent. Ultimately, it is healthy that both of you foster quality relationships. A mindful way of approaching your child having quality time is visualizing your child having a positive experience during the shared time together. Visualize your child smiling and feeling connected with your coparent. Take the time to visualize yourself feeling connected and joyous with your child.

You can add a cue word that that will prompt you to visualize a positive image. Practice the visualization three times a day for a month and notice the difference.

GRATITUDE

Sharing appreciations for specific things that your coparent does for your children, or for you personally, helps foster a respectful working partnership. It takes great effort, consciousness, and attention to raise your children well, and it is important to recognize and appreciate what you are both doing to meet that goal. Effective coparenting can easily go unacknowledged, and when you choose to verbally acknowledge your coparent, you are making a positive bid for a connection that helps invest in your future interactions and good will toward one another. The key to practicing gratitude with your coparent is having the acknowledgment be genuine and specific. Avoid blanket statements such as "You are the best" because it is a broad statement of praise, and your coparent can easily discount it. Areas that are worthwhile to acknowledge should encompass her parenting skills, her character around your child, or how you have felt supported by your coparent.

A gratitude practice is also an effective exercise to release negativity from prior experiences in the relationship. If you feel like it would be too difficult to verbalize gratitudes, then start with writing a few daily in a journal format. Practicing gratitude provides an amazing connection with what is good right now in the present moment. Write gratitudes in the present tense with affirming positive language; they should be devoid of negatives or double negatives. Some examples of gratitude statements are:

O I am grateful that my children have both parents in their lives.

O I am grateful that my coparent is able to consistently pick up the kids on time as we agreed.

O I am grateful that our children feel loved and supported by both of us.

- I am grateful that I have a coparent to share parenting responsibilities with.

- I am grateful for how my coparent is able to be so patient with our youngest.

- I am grateful for how my coparent was able to switch nights so I could go to my social function, which made feel supported.

Gratitude is a contagious act. The more you practice gratitude, the more your eyes are open to seeing things in your life to be grateful for. Gratitude changes perspective on situations and relationships, and in turn changes the dynamics of relationships.

POLITENESS

The act of being polite and acknowledging each other, particularly in front of your children, helps keep the climate between you and your coparent cordial. Being polite is also a reparative gesture with your coparent that models to your children that you can choose how you behave. Remembering that you both have little people in common, who are the most important people in your life, can be a reset button to remain more polite if this has been a problem area in the past.

KINDNESS

An act of kindness for your coparent is an act of appreciation, and it can involve your children. Helping your children remember birthdays and holiday gifts for your coparent actually benefits your children in learning how to think of others. Inviting your coparent over to dinner for shared occasions with the kids is also a demonstration of kindness and putting the relationships with your children first. If you are aware of a health issue, or a difficult circumstance that has arisen for your coparent, have the conversation on how you can support your coparent's parenting responsibilities, if possible. Being kind to one of the most important people in your child's life is an act of love for you child.

Important Points to Consider

Fostering mutual respect with your coparent is essential. Here are some reflections to help you create an amiable coparenting atmosphere:

- Practicing respect with your coparent happens in small ways and builds over time.

- A little kindness can go a long way in your coparenting relationship. Staying positive with one another starts with you. Don't wait for the other person to start being positive. You support your child feeling more comfortable when you are kind.

- If you hold onto past resentments, take the time to work on them and free yourself.

- Remember the Golden Rule: Treat others as you want to be treated.

CHAPTER 11

Know Your Rights As a Conscious Coparent

Coparenting arrangements are essential in providing a framework for how you will coparent together. When figuring out your ideal arrangement, you have to look at all the options and understand your legal rights. Discussions must happen on priority topics, such as your child's education, health, and religion. It's important to decide ahead of time what agreements you will continue to follow for your child. Do your best to keep as much as possible consistent, but if you have to make changes because of moving or finances, then allow time for your child to adjust. Deciding where your children will live and how much time they will spend with each of you is equally important, as is how you will resolve any parenting issues that come up in the future. This chapter will address the essential topics to cover your legal rights and the types of custody arrangements that make sense for conscious coparents.

Types of Custody

Several types of custody arrangements apply to all couples who share the custody of a child. This also includes two people who had a baby together without being married. You both have rights as coparents regardless of not being legally married. Let's look at the different types.

LEGAL CUSTODY

Legal custody is when one parent has the sole decision-making skills around health, education, and religion. Legal custody does not always mean you have sole physical custody of your child, but it does mean that you are the primary decision-maker for your child, and often a parent with sole legal custody also has the sole physical custody of a child.

Most parents in family court are awarded joint legal custody. If you share joint legal custody, then you can choose to divide up the major decisions, for example one parent chooses which school the child attends, while the other makes health and wellness decisions. When legal decisions come in conflict, coparents have to reflect on how their decision-making is impacting their child.

For example, Donna and Jason both share legal custody of Owen and have decided to divide the decisions of health and education. Donna is the healthcare decision-maker and Jason is the education decision-maker. Jason chose a school for Owen that had high academic standards. He was excited about it because he felt Owen was very smart and could benefit from a more rigorous curriculum. A couple of months into the program, Owen no longer seemed to enjoy school, had difficulty paying attention in class, and was presenting with anxiety about going to school. Donna had been observing Owen's changing behavior around school and thought it was affecting him psychologically, so she took him to see a child therapist. The child therapist confirmed that the academic environment was affecting his self-esteem because Owen was anxious about not being able to keep up with the rest of his class. At this point, Donna and Jason were not working with each other, but most importantly, they were not working with Owen.

If you decide to divide the major decisions for your child between the two of you, then also consider adding in an addendum that you both have the ability to re-evaluate decisions if they potentially mentally, emotionally, or physically cause harm to the child. Certain agreements that were good ideas for the child at a certain age may have to change at a different age stage.

PHYSICAL CUSTODY

Physical custody is when either one parent or both parents have the right to have their child live with him or her. The court awards joint physical custody, or decides in a custody agreement that the child can spend significant amounts of time with both parents. Joint physical custody is ideal when parents live relatively close to each other, and the child can live at least 40 percent of the time with one of the parents. Joint physical custody is also ideal for children at grade-school level because it reduces stress and allows for a somewhat normal routine between both homes. Younger children are often better off remaining in one home for the majority of the time so their routines are not overwhelmed.

JOINT CUSTODY

Joint custody is when both parents share legal and physical custody. This is an ideal custody arrangement for conscious coparents because you are both willing to be equally involved in the decisions of parenting and be consistently available.

Coparenting Living Arrangements

There are many questions to consider when deciding the ideal living arrangement for your child. Most people think in terms of the best interests of the child, but you also have to consider what is financially feasible for you to sustain. For some coparents, it may be sustainable to maintain a living arrangement for the first year of divorce and then transition living arrangements at a later date. Whatever you decide, consider the following:

- **The age and developmental stage of your children:** The younger the child, the more routine will be required. Younger children typically need to be in the custody of a primary caregiver.

- **Any special needs your children may have:** Special needs, whether a disability, chronic health issues, learning disorders, sensory issues, and so on, are all areas to evaluate when deciding the ideal living arrangement for the child. Parents need to choose the home that can provide the optimum care for the child's needs and can most adequately meet these needs with care and emotional support. With some special needs like chronic health issues, it may be in the better interests of the child to remain at one home, and then have visitation from the other parent, or take the necessary time to set up both homes to provide adequately for your child's needs.

- **Your children's relationship with each parent:** Having a connected relationship with each parent is important, and creating a schedule that supports both parents having adequate time to nurture their relationship is key.

- **Your children's relationship with siblings, grandparents, and extended family:** Having ample time with grandparents, aunts, uncles, and cousins in a coparenting arrangement supports your child's relationship with her extended family. These relationships are important to the people in your child's world, and you want to ensure that your child has access to them. Consider extending part of your shared time on occasions to visit the grandparents or to see cousins.

- **Care arrangements prior to separation:** If you had a nanny, daycare, or regular babysitter before the separation or divorce, your child's relationship with the caregiver may provide some constancy during the coparenting transition. A caregiver who has been a part of the development of your child is part of your child's support network. It's also helpful to have someone close to the family offer observations about how your child is handling the transition to coparenting, and maybe even fill in the gaps with your child as needed.

Separation and divorce can be a time of emotional preoccupation, and having loving and supportive caregivers can truly help with the transition.

○ **Your children's wishes:** Children in their preteens and teens should have a say about their living arrangements, providing either parent is not coercing their opinions. As your children get older, their social relationships and school functions grow increasingly more important to them. Conscious coparents take into account their children's preferences and, and if possible, honor them. Ultimately, you are the parent, and if you and your coparent find that it is not feasible, then empathetically share the reasons for your decision. When it comes to the wishes of smaller children, listen to their wishes and really hear their needs.

○ **Each parent's parenting abilities:** There are ages that are easier for one parent and prove more difficult for the other, and vice versa. Consider what you are both good at with the kids based on their current needs. Make adjustments as needed to give your kids the best support you both can offer. In order to do this, you have to be humble enough to recognize areas in your parenting that are challenging. Evaluating your challenges requires vulnerability. If you have a strong coparenting relationship, it may be possible to share these challenges without fear of retribution. Conscious coparents who work effectively together can trust that the other parent is doing his best and means well. For example, the baby stage may be very difficult for one parent, while the grade-school years may be an ideal time for this parent.

○ **The safety of each parent:** If a parent has significant deficits and they put your child at risk, then you have to take steps to protect your child. Such areas of concern are alcohol or drug addiction, physical and/or sexual abuse, neglect, and mental illness. This also includes if the parent is living or remarried to someone who is behaving in any of these ways around the child. You need to protect your child, and taking legal action is a necessity.

The stronger your ability to communicate as coparents, the more effective you will be, and your children will feel the difference. Research shows it's not necessarily divorce that affects children; it is how the parents treat one another and the level of conflict witnessed by the children. Truly, people who divorce or separate can coparent well if they take the time to personally grieve any hurts outside the coparenting relationship.

Coparents of children with special needs should look at ways to support the primary coparent from caregiver burnout. Use the visitation schedule for both coparents to divide responsibilities as much as possible, and look to your support network for ways they can contribute.

TYPES OF LIVING ARRANGEMENTS TO EXPLORE

There are many options to choose from when it comes to coparenting living arrangements. You want to choose an arrangement that will provide optimum time with both parents; one that creates a routine that your children can adapt to.

Freeman Order

Since the mid-1970s and '80s, the Freeman order has been standard practice for custody arrangements. The Freeman order is alternating weekends for the noncustodial parent to have time with the children from Friday to Sunday every other week, and one night over during the middle of the week. The logic behind the Freeman order is not to interfere with the child's school schedule as much as possible. Overnights in the middle of the week typically work better because since it is the mid-point of the week, it provides a touch point with the noncustodial parent every week. It is very important to have weekly contact on the weeks when the noncustodial parent does not have visitation. This arrangement is still a popular choice in living arrangements.

Day On, Day Off

This arrangement is where parents share time with their kids in an every-other-day schedule. For some children this can work, but for many children traveling back and forth between homes, this can be difficult.

One Week On, One Week Off

In this arrangement, coparents share their time in block schedules of one week with the transition happening typically on Sundays prior to the start of the school week. The pros of this schedule are that you get a full week with your child and can get a solid rhythm for your household with each other. It can also work well if you have a job where you travel frequently and can schedule the off weeks for your travel. The downside of this schedule is that you get two weeks off per month that can feel lonely for you and for your children. If you have children who are sensitive to not seeing you more regularly, then consider another option. A variation of this schedule for coparents is one parent can be in charge for that week, but the other coparent is available and helping with pickups, homework, etc. Once again, assess both the child's needs and what the coparents are comfortable with.

2-2-5-5 Plan

This plan is a trendier custody arrangement in the courts. Both parents have fifty-fifty physical custody, with an arrangement of two days on, two days off, five days on, five days off. One parent has physical custody of the children for two consecutive days from drop-off at school on Monday morning (8:00 A.M. if there is no school on Monday) until drop-off at school on Wednesday morning (8:00 A.M. if there is no school on Wednesday). The other coparent has physical custody of the children for the next two consecutive days from drop-off at school on Wednesday morning (8:00 A.M. if there is no school on Wednesday) until drop-off at school on Friday morning (8:00 A.M. if there is no school on Friday). Then the coparents alternate weekend custody, with the weekend custody arrangement beginning at drop-off at school on Friday morning (8:00 A.M. if there is no school on Friday) until drop-off at school on Monday morning (8:00 A.M. if there is no school on Monday). This way parents are able to have five consecutive days with their child.

The positive aspects for coparents who practice this arrangement are that their children will be able to have equal time with both parents and have the ability to develop a rhythm with each of their parents in both home environments. There are coparenting arrangements where one parent has longer work hours and is able to work out with the other coparent an after-school schedule where the noncustodial parent handles pickups and after-school functions for the children until the custodial parent gets off work. If both parents work, they should agree on a caregiver or daycare. Ideally, both parents would use it to create more consistency for their child. For some coparents, the upside to this arrangement is also having a little communication between the coparents during pickups and drop-offs. Being able to communicate with your coparent is still important in raising your children well together in your coparenting partnership. Find time outside of pickups and drop-offs to touch base on what is happening for your children.

LIVING SITUATIONS

Once you both decide on your parenting agreement, your living situations can have different looks. There is one option of having the child live separately between two homes. In this arrangement, your child has two different homes. She shares one home with you and another home with her other parent. Your child will have the opportunity to have two different bedrooms and adjust to two different households.

The other living situation option is bird nesting. Bird nesting is when the children remain in the home and the parents take turns staying in the home. This way, the children's lives are not interrupted by the transition of having to move. This is especially beneficial for smaller children and for children who are very attached to their homes. The downside of bird nesting is that it may be cost prohibitive because you typically have to pay rent or have mortgages for three locations (two separate living spaces for both coparents outside of the home), and for many families, this is not financially feasible.

Choosing the ideal living arrangement for you and your family has to work for everyone. Whatever you decide and implement with your coparent, the kids will get used to it, and will adjust based on how they see you adjusting as well.

Coparenting Agreements

It is current practice in family court to refer to child visitation as shared time because it feels offensive for coparents who are actively involved in their child's lives to refer to their time as a visitation. Shared time feels more appropriate because as coparents, you are sharing the daily responsibilities of raising your children together.

Parents can work on their own custody arrangements without having attorneys represent them, but it depends on the people and the personalities involved in the decision-making process. If you have an effective working relationship where your child's needs come first and both coparents want to work together, then it may work out for you to come to your own agreement. There are online resources where you can pay a nominal fee for all the paperwork you would need to file with the family courts on your own. Coparents who have been parenting a significant amount of time may have already come to an easier coparenting agreement. If you have been married for a while and the routine for your family is well developed, then coparenting using this same routine may still be an option. If both parties are willing to work out what is in the best interests of the children, planning the living arrangements, logistics, holidays, and life issues for the kids can be easier. However, it is in both of your interests to take what you have agreed on to a mediator or family law attorney to make your decisions legal and binding. You can add into your legal document that you will both try working out parenting arrangements with each other before considering legal action.

MEDIATION

Mediation is when a neutral third party who is typically a licensed psychotherapist and/or attorney mediates the negotiation of custody and finances between coparents. Mediation may be a more cost effective approach for divorce for coparents who wish to work on their parenting agreement. It may be effective for couples who feel they can work things out more equitably between each other rather than going to court. A mediator does not take sides and cannot give legal advice to either party involved. A mediator helps by asking thoughtful questions and creating a neutral safe space for both parties. Attorneys who are mediators can file the divorce proceedings or the parenting settlements. Mediation may not be the most advantageous solution when an ex-partner intimidates the other individual.

SEEKING LEGAL REPRESENTATION

Seeking legal representation, rather than seeking mediation, is typically the best option when there is a more dominant personality and a more passive personality in a relationship. Often, personalities that are more dominant lay out the plan they want for the settlement and custody arrangement and get the outcome they desire. This leaves the more passive individual often feeling like he didn't advocate well enough for himself. Problems also arise in mediation when two dominant personalities cannot compromise. When embarking upon negotiations on custody arrangements, you want to know the full extent of your rights. The only way you can advocate for your rights is to seek legal representation. There is a saying that "People end up hiring attorneys who are reflective of their own tone and personality." For example, an aggressive person will often hire an aggressive attorney. Finding legal representation that aligns with your value system and what you want for your life with your children is essential. You want an attorney who is representing you, protecting your parental rights, and educating you on what your rights are.

Legal representation for coparents deciding on custody arrangements is just as important as it is for coparents approaching custody during a divorce proceeding. Coparents have the same parental rights as married couples. If you started off having a friendly relationship deciding on visitation, then take the steps to solidify what you agreed on by legally documenting your decisions. Stress and psychosocial factors can change how a person negotiates, and it is best to take the time now to prepare both of you for the expectations set forth in the coparenting relationship.

The added benefit of retaining a family law attorney is that she will outline everything in your custody arrangement for both parties going forward, and you have a legally binding document that asserts the rules of your coparenting arrangement. Custody documents can extensively cover the rules and procedures of custody, including the following:

O Parents will cooperate with one another.

O Children are not conduits, meaning the "go between" for the parents.

O No derogatory remarks about the other parent in front of the children.

O Pickup and drop-off times.

O Vacation schedule.

O Protocol for managing social invitations for your child, particularly when events are scheduled on your coparent's scheduled time.

O Share all information pertinent to the child's schedule, including academics, extracurricular activities, health, and wellness.

O Access to school and healthcare records.

O Mutual consent for healthcare, passports, and education.

This list is a highlighted version of what most family attorneys will include in an agreement. You can't anticipate everything when you are creating a custody settlement, and there are things that will come up where you may have to make amendments. Even with a court document outlining all of your coparenting protocols, you may still need to go back to court to handle specific issues if you need to advocate for your children's protection and/or care. For parents who demonstrate the ability to communicate and work things out, you can write into your agreement that you both can amend the agreement if you mutually agree to do so.

Hiring a legal representative may seem costly to you. It can range in the thousands of dollars to pay for legal representation, but the long-term benefits of securing a legal plan for your custody arrangement are priceless. You can pursue how to proceed with each other by hiring a sole practitioner instead of a family attorney from a large legal firm. This form of counsel can also help cut costs, and potentially she may be more available to answer questions. Family attorneys who are sole practitioners, meaning they are not part of a larger firm with significant overhead, tend to have a sense of purpose with their clients. They can be good family lawyers for both parties.

Choose an attorney you feel comfortable representing you. It is common for people to select a lawyer based on how similar he or she is to them. It is also important that you feel very confident in her organizational and assertion skills. After all, the attorney you choose is handling a major part of your life.

CONSIDERATIONS FOR CONSCIOUS COPARENTS

You may find yourself in a positive relationship with your coparent because you are able to focus on the needs of your children first, and you genuinely like and appreciate your coparent. If this is the case, both of you can map out the ideal schedule, custody arrangement, and financial plan for the kids. The benefits of having a viable conscious coparenting relationship are that you are modeling to your child what being a secure connector is and that you love and support your child first over any past or personal issues with your coparent.

Even if you have a great relationship with your coparent, take the time to go to an attorney and draw up a custody agreement. It is worth the investment and creates a structure to your relationship that benefits everyone in the long run. You can always change it if, at a certain point, it no longer works.

You can offer this powerful legacy to your children. If your relationship is amenable and you consider yourself friends, consider the following.

Work Schedules to Be Present for the Kids

You will have to figure out how you will both make two different homes work financially. Some coparents would rather have the children continue to live in their homes and then work together to maintain and care for the kids, or have the kids come home after school to the coparent who is able to pick them up from school and get homework and after-school activities completed. This plan typically works until there is a significant relationship for one of the coparents, but it can continue to work if both parties' significant others understand and respect how you and your coparent have set up your child rearing. If you have a parent who is available after school and wants to be there for the kids, then it makes sense to allow that parent to be there for the children, rather than use a daycare provider who will not have the same level of care as a parent.

You can ask for a first right of refusal during your coparent's shared time for after-school pickups, so it is not outsourced to a daycare provider unless necessary.

Share Vacations

Some conscious coparents who have strong parenting partnerships are able to continue taking vacations as a family. Evaluate if this is something you could commit to. The upside to being able to share vacations with your coparent is that your children can continue to foster positive memories with the two of you, even if you are no longer together. Shared vacations can also demonstrate to your children that you are still friends with your ex. Children can bear the burden of divorce much easier if there is little conflict in the coparenting relationship, and if they witness you both continuing to like one another. Consider shared vacations only if you have a viable friendship, because you don't want to spend vacations arguing and fighting one another.

Most coparents split holidays evenly as agreed to by both parties. The courts can also order holiday division in the event the parties are not able to reach an agreement. Each coparent typically has up to two weeks of vacation with their children during summer vacation, either consecutively or at different points during the summer break. In the event of a scheduling conflict, coparents typically decide who will have priority during odd years, and the other coparent has priority for vacation times on the even years.

Spend Time at Each Other's Homes During Holidays

It is possible to share the holidays as coparents to support your children feeling connected to both of you during these special occasions. Coparents who make this work respect the need for individual space at holidays, but also keep in mind that their children would ideally not want to divide time with their parents on the holidays. Conscious coparents who value how their children experience the holidays look for appropriate ways to include each other. For example, conscious coparents Megan and Nathan both remarried and had a strong coparenting partnership. Both Megan and Nathan felt strongly about including each parent in their son's holiday experience. Each year they would switch the holiday schedules where Joshua would wake up and open presents. Then the other coparent would host Christmas lunch for family and friends at their home, and Joshua's other coparent and stepparent would join.

Important Points to Consider

Invest in putting together a legal document outlining your coparenting agreement. The document will help address the general structure of your arrangement, and as coparents, you can be flexible with one another on a case-by-case basis. Consider the following:

- Choose a custody situation that best fits the developmental needs of your children.
- Consult with an attorney on all the important factors that matter to you in a parenting agreement. Your family law attorney should already be well aware of the kind of requests you can write into an agreement.

○ If you have a positive working relationship with your coparent, consider being progressive in sharing holidays or even family vacations together.

○ Choose living arrangements and education based on what you both can financially manage. Your children will emotionally do better with coparents who are not constantly financially stressed.

**CHAPTER 12**

Discipline When Coparenting

Disciplining your child in two different homes can be one of the more contentious areas of a coparenting relationship. Coparents who see discipline differently often want to parent differently, and this can cause mixed messages for children in a variety of areas. From a conscious coparenting perspective, you ultimately want your child to know that both parents love him no matter what. Limits are set out of love and deep care for the child, not a punitive approach. This chapter will reflect on the challenges in disciplining differently, and then it will look at an approach that is more reflective of a conscious coparenting form of discipline.

Discipline Is a Practice

As authors Tina Payne Bryson and Dr. Dan Siegel wrote in *No-Drama Discipline*, "The goal in discipline is to teach." Discipline is a practice. It is not something that is mastered in the moment, but something that must be practiced again and again and again. It is better to look at this as a process—a long-term approach to teaching your child how to be in the world. As a coparent, sometimes you will get it right, sometimes you will get it wrong. Sometimes you may question if your coparent could have handled it differently and could have done a better job with the situation. Sometimes when you mishandle a discipline moment, it leads you to getting it right the next time, or learning something else about yourself or your child. Seeing discipline as a practice may offer you the compassion you need when challenges arise.

Evaluate how you are doing with your own self-care. Are you going to bed on time and getting enough sleep? Are you learning the discipline of saying no to others? Are you managing your life with rhythm and routine? Are you meeting your own needs? It can make a difference in your ability to parent or discipline when one of these areas is not functioning well.

CONSCIOUS DISCIPLINE STARTS WITH CONSCIOUS SELF-DISCIPLINE

Effectively disciplining your children requires the ability to set limits. Your own ability to know your personal limits, and how to care for yourself, is essential. Your ability to get sufficient rest, eat well, get sufficient exercise, and handle personal stress all factor into your ability to manage your children while disciplining. This is so because when you have adequate self-care, you are replenished enough psychologically and emotionally to stay present when you're with your children. Discipline moments can often escalate because of how the parent is handling the situation rather than how the child is behaving.

Conscious coparents who align on disciplining similarly will have a more coherent and organized positive discipline structure because the goal is to remain a secure connector while disciplining your child.

Differing Discipline

You may have a discipline challenge that is different from your coparent and you are scratching your head and wondering why your child behaves this way with just you. Misbehavior happens for a variety of reasons, and in coparenting situations, you need to evaluate if any of the misbehaviors are associated to the different relationship your child has with each coparent, or if it is attributed to the divorce or separation. When a child misbehaves in one house instead of the other house, it may be because the child has a different attachment style and relationship with each parent. Children who feel insecure about a parent's love may be better behaved or compliant because they want to please and show their worthwhileness for loving. Alternatively, a child who has the freedom to act out at home and misbehave at times, may feel secure enough in the parental relationship to do so.

THE THREE MAIN PARENTING STYLES

Another challenge for coparents is when they use vastly different discipline styles. There is much literature on the three main parenting styles of authoritarian, permissive, and authoritative.

○ **Authoritarian** parenting is when the parent dictates what is best for the child and usually links discipline to punishment.

○ **Permissive** parenting is when the parent lets the child get away with misbehavior, and is often not consistent with discipline because he does not want to upset the child.

○ **Authoritative** parenting is an approach where the parent blends setting limits and working with the child to understand the misbehavior in a caring manner, keeping the attachment intact.

Imagine how different parenting styles create conflict in coparenting partnerships. For example, one coparent sees discipline from the authoritarian perspective and tries to control the child through punishments first, while an authoritative parent empowers the child with a voice and mediates the misbehavior with logical consequence. The previous examples are two different messages around discipline. A child will often feel more emotionally connected with a parent who is authoritative than authoritarian. Differing parenting styles can also cause older children and teens to not share as much when there are serious problems because the child will fear having privileges taken away. Ultimately, you want your child to respect your setting limits, not be scared of them to the point of withholding pertinent information. This is particularly serious once your child is a teenager and the repercussions can have life-changing effects.

PARENTING STYLE REPERCUSSIONS

Different parenting styles can also cause a child to prefer one home to the other. This is common with permissive homes. If a coparent is more permissive rather than authoritarian, there is a likelihood that the child may like visiting this parent because of what he can get away with. The goal for a permissive parent is to keep the child happy. Happy is a short-term pursuit as a parenting goal, and it does not foster a longer-term vision for resilience and self-correction. Some permissive parents may mistake their child being happy for feeling more connected to the parent. If you find yourself trying to make your child happy because you feel guilty you divorced or are not able to coparent in the same house, then consider the true cost of your guilt. For most permissive parents, the costs breaks down into lack of effective boundaries, ability to remain consistent, and perhaps the message that you don't think your child is capable of hearing "no" from you. If you find yourself relating to this, take the time to reflect on what need you are meeting personally when relating to your children more permissively.

Parenting is not about keeping kids happy all the time. Parenting is about fostering an effective connection between parent and child, and raising your child to be a self-correcting adult. How you discipline plays a major part in raising your children effectively, and it needs to be intertwined with connecting with your child first, about how she is feeling, before you can correct the behavior.

A Conscious Coparent Wisely HALTS

Before implementing your discipline approach, you have to ask yourself where your child's behavior may be coming from. When children misbehave, it often stems from the simple to the very complex. Speak with your coparent about any patterns you may both see in your child, the frequency of behavior, and if there are commonalities, like a certain point in the day and triggers for your child for misbehavior. Using HALTS will help you better assess how to address discipline issues with your child.

Parents who use HALTS are able to address the real limit-setting issues with their child more effectively than getting into entrenched battles that originate from being hungry or overtired. Rule out the origins of the misbehavior using the conscious coparenting HALTS technique:

H: HUNGRY

Some children can become very irritable and behave regrettably when overly hungry. Many parents comment that there is a witching hour in their homes from the hours of 4–6 P.M. in the evening when children's bellies are getting ready for dinner. You can say the same for parents who may not have had even a sufficient lunch, and dinner may be the only decent meal of their day. Hungry kids do not have the glucose in their brains to feed their concentration, and this can cause more tantrums. If you have a child who struggles with misbehavior when hungry, implement the following:

O Serve frequent nutritious smaller meals throughout the day.

O Set up a healthy appetizer you are comfortable with your child having while waiting for dinner to get ready, like carrots and hummus, cheese and crackers, nuts.

○ Keeping children who misbehave frequently hydrated is also an easy way to help. Adequate hydration helps the brain and overall body function better.

○ A smaller nourishing snack before bed for children, like oatmeal or almond butter, can help children sleep better, and it is not difficult for the body to digest.

Help to rule out misbehavior due to being overly hungry by having snacks available in the car after school, during pickup, or for longer rides in the car. Drop off your child to your coparent after feeding her a nutritious meal to help reduce irritability during the transition.

A: ANGRY

Angry children will demonstrate their anger through tantrums and misbehavior. Your job as a parent is to climb the "cognitive tree" of your child's brain to figure out what's causing the angry reaction. Climbing your child's cognitive tree means helping your child figure out what or how she is thinking about that is causing her to feel so angry. You can only get to this information provided you are nonreactive yourself. If you approach the problem from a calmer state, you will help your child regulate faster. Your key tool to understanding your child's angry behavior is attuning to what your child is feeling and connecting about it. Connecting first about your child's feelings has to happen before you set further limits about the repercussions of your child' behavior. Behavior that started from feeling angry and resulted in destruction of toys or property, name-calling, or cruelty will need a limit set. Plan to set the limit after your child has calmed down.

L: LONELY

Frequently lonely children often have discipline issues because children display depressive symptoms in ways that are more aggressive rather than lying in bed and pulling over the covers. Loneliness for a child is a painful feeling because it is also tied to her self-esteem. When a child feels lonely because of lack of friends, or missing time with loved ones, it feels personal and like there is something wrong with them. Attuning to your child feeling lonely should be met with sensitivity. There are instances for children where their loneliness stems from lack of school relationships, and understanding your children's world at school will be important to grasp. Older children and teens need their parents to really listen about what the loneliness is like for them. Come up with a plan on how to rectify the situation if possible.

T: TIRED

Overtired children will often misbehave more and making sure your child is getting adequate rest at both homes is important. If you have a little one who is chronically misbehaving toward bedtime, it may be that he is very tired and needs to go to bed earlier. Using discipline tools like taking away privileges or time-outs for children who are overly tired only escalates the misbehavior. Address the misbehavior by resting, or finding time later in the day for your child to rest. Tiredness can affect academics, school play, sports, and home life. Some children truly need more sleep than others need. Evaluate the following:

O How much sleep is your child getting based on his age and development? Is it enough?

O Does your child's day have downtime interspersed throughout his day? Keeping a fast clip to the day can create chronic tiredness and adrenal depletion.

O For older kids and teens, is there any use of highly caffeinated energy drinks or coffee drinks?

S: SICK

Children who are sick with a cold can often have misbehavior issues because they are grumpy and don't feel good. Sickness can also cause a lack of concentration and a short temper because it takes so much effort to be thoughtful with your words. If your child fits in this category, this is when you prepare for a day of caring for your sick child and slow his schedule down so he can recuperate.

Don't Always Follow Your First Reaction

When disciplining in the moment with your child, you may get really upset. This "gut reaction" in the moment may prompt you to react rather than respond to your child in a mature way. These gut reactions in the moment can come from an implicit childhood memory or experience related to your own family of origin issue. Sometimes your knee-jerk reaction is the way you were raised, and you haven't reflected enough about how you were disciplined to know if you even want to behave this way. For this reason, your gut can't always be trusted as the most effective immediate response to your child's behavior. Rather, see the gut reaction as an alarm that lets you know that you need to reflect on what you are feeling because your reaction feels bigger than what the circumstances are calling for.

LET YOUR KIDS FAIL

In effective discipline, there are occasions where you find your child misbehaving and you have to follow through on consequences, even if you could let him slide just one more time. The downside to the proverbial slide is that your child won't learn anything out of this teaching moment.

For example, say your child has been chronically forgetting to bring her homework to school. You get to school and your child looks at you and asks you to go back home and get her homework for her. If you go back and get her homework, she won't experience the natural consequence of not having her homework in class, or how her teacher will manage that problem. You lovingly tell your daughter that you understand her situation and that it may feel stressful to her that she doesn't have her homework with her. Then you tell her that you will not be able to go back home to get her homework. By setting this limit, your child has the opportunity to take personal responsibility for her problem. She can then come up with a better solution of bringing her homework to school in the future.

That's a big teaching moment packaged in a small exchange. Yet it can have lasting results when you don't save your child from her mistakes and are loving with your limit. In the practice of discipline, you sometimes must allow your children to fail and understand that this is part of their growth. It is also a part of your growth as a parent.

Coparents who offer mixed messages of saving their children from feeling the repercussions of their own mistakes need to evaluate where their intentions are coming from. Most often, it is because the parent cannot bear to see the child hurting. Coparents who feel guilty about divorce may have more difficulty with saving because they feel their child has had to endure so much already, so helping along the way should be acceptable. There may be some truth to being helpful, but look at how often you are helping and who is it really helping—you or your child?

MANAGE YOUR OWN FEELINGS

Children can trigger anger for parents when they are disciplining. Learning how to take a break and walk away from a heated moment with your child is a good idea if you feel like you are not going to handle the situation well.

When upset with your child, think in terms of "better to do no harm." It's perfectly okay if you need to take a break. If you have a history of childhood abuse or anger management issues, giving yourself the space to process before you discipline is key. Gather your thoughts before you approach so you can be in a better headspace.

When you discipline effectively, you have to be willing to take the proverbial "hit" with your child. This may look like being willing to leave an entire cart of groceries at the store if your child is busting out a little Nero tantrum. It could also look like having to leave a playdate early in front of other parents and children because your child is misbehaving. Your child's misbehavior is not a complete reflection of you as a person or parent. Your child's misbehavior is a reflection of a dysregulated state that doesn't know any other way to be understood than to be off-putting. Support yourself with friendships that understand what you are trying to work on with your child.

Case Study: Bella

Jenny and Roger had a little five-year-old girl named Bella who was transitioning to being coparented by Jenny primarily during the school week and seeing her dad on Wednesdays and weekends. Bella had started kindergarten, and her teacher shared with Jenny that Bella was having a hard time making friends. One of Bella's particular problems was that she wanted to control all the play with her friends, and when it came to toys, she did not want to share. Her mom thought it would be a good idea to invite some of the little girls over for a playdate in order to practice how to share and play along with the other children's ideas. In preparation for the playdate, Jenny called and invited three other moms to attend. She let them know ahead of time that Jenny would be working with Bella on learning how to share, so there might be a moment where Jenny would have to excuse Bella from the playtime in order to correct the behavior. The moms appreciated Jenny's proactivity with Bella and even felt inspired to join in the lesson on sharing with their girls. Then Jenny took a little time each day before the playdate to role-play with Bella on how to share. Bella decided ahead of time what toys she would bring out to play with, and what special toys she would put away during the playdate. Jenny set the limit that whatever toys were out, Bella had to let everyone choose the toys they wanted to play with before she did because Jenny wanted her daughter to experience being a gracious hostess to her friends.

Jenny let her coparent Roger know the news she had received from Bella's teacher; she also told him what she was planning to practice at home. Roger joined in the role-play on his day with Bella and pretended to be a friend at the playdate who had his own ideas on how to play with some of her toys. Bella richly enjoyed her father pretending with her.

At the playdate, Bella did an excellent job of letting her friends pick toys first and asking to trade toys as the afternoon went on. About an hour into the play, Bella started to get upset that the girls did not want to play her way with some of the dolls. Jenny excused Bella and herself to the other room to attune to her feelings and told Bella she could stay in her room if she wanted, or she could rejoin her friends for the playdate and perhaps offer a different idea to play or hear what the other girls wanted to try. Jenny also offered a craft for the girls in case they wanted something else to do instead. Bella decided to rejoin the group because she really wanted to be with her friends rather than stay in her room. Once she rejoined, the girls decided the craft was a great idea, so they got involved with their moms on a fun beaded necklace project.

The two hours were successful for Bella, and Jenny felt proud of how she and Roger had handled the situation collectively because it was her first obstacle in her coparenting relationship with Roger to see how they could work together. Roger and Jenny looked forward to seeing if it made a difference in the classroom for Bella. The level of support Bella received from both Jenny and Roger did help her share more effectively and resulted in a behavior change in her classroom.

If your child says, "I hate you" after a limit has been set, calmly say something to the effect, "Sounds like you are feeling pretty hurt about the limit Mom/Dad had to set." Sharing that the words hurt you, or displaying a reaction of shock, only adds more fuel to the fire in the moment. Once your child is calm, you can return to this earlier remark and discuss how words hurt and discuss a more effective way for your child to handle when he is upset.

TOLERATE BEING DISLIKED

For some coparents, it can be anxiety provoking for your kids not to like you, because you do not want your kids to like you less than they do your coparent. This is particularly tough during the teenage years when you may have to tolerate this feeling for significant periods. Remember, your child dislikes the limit being set and may not be able to distinguish between the limit setting and the parent. Most children do not like limits, even though they are vital to growth. As a conscious coparent, you have to hold the long-term vision for how you want to raise your child. It is in these moments that you let the comment roll off your back and don't take it personally. This is even if your child says, "I hate you." Disregard the statement and do not put energy toward it because your child will know that his words affected you, and then he will use the statement again at another time. This just means that your child is very angry and hurt about the limit, but it does not necessarily mean that he really hates you. Tolerating your child's big feelings is a sign of maturity and strength in your parenting.

Conscious Coparenting Keeps Discipline Consistent

Even if you and your coparent have different parenting styles, remaining united on the major points of discipline help give a constant message to your children. You can approach this message differently based on your own temperament and parenting style, but the message should remain the same. A simple way to approach the values you have for your home is to have a set of house rules listed. Coparents can have different rules in their homes, but consider aligning on the priority rules with your coparent so you have a consistent message for your child. For example, house rules may include five rules that speak about the positive behaviors you expect. Here are five rules to consider, but feel free to use rules that speak to you and your household:

O Practice being kind with your words to one another

O Practice gentle hands with each other

O If you use an item that belongs to someone else, ask first and put it away after

O When necessary, be willing to talk out problems once you cool down

O Practice helpfulness

Choosing house rules and then reviewing them with your child are important because you need "buy in" from your child. Review what the house rules are with your children on a semi-regular basis. Here is an example of how to use the house rules on a child who used poor language at home because she wanted to go out with friends instead of doing homework. This technique is called RAP.

1. **Refer:** Begin by referring to the rule: "Sydney, using kind words is one of our house rules, and I am noticing you are not following one of the rules right now."

2. **Attune:** Attune to what your child is feeling: "You seem frustrated right now about not being able to go with your friend. I know friends are really important to you, and your homework is also important."

3. **Problem Solve:** Problem solve by asking your child what her plan would be: "Can you share with me how you plan to take care of this predicament?"

Discipline Tools

It's easy to get carried away with any discipline approach when you are parenting out of anger or are emotionally triggered. It is important with any discipline approach you use to ask yourself, "What do I want my child to learn through this?" Shaming and humiliating your child to get to the end result will only create long-term consequences. Here are some helpful tools that originate from a more positive discipline approach.

REDIRECTION

The act of redirection is to hear your child's want and to attune to it, but then redirect it to something that may be a good substitute. For example, your child wants to buy a toy at the grocery store when you only want to buy groceries. You would redirect your child in the following way: "That is a really fun toy. I can imagine you might really enjoy playing with that bouncy ball. Let's put this toy on your wish list so we can remember when it's time to buy you something special. Notice that the statement did not start with a "no" because hearing the word "no" often is off-putting and actually turns on negative receptors in the brain. Putting a positive twist on your redirect helps your child accept it. Your child may still be whiny about not having the toy right away, but if the choice is to have it later or not have it at all, which would you choose? Using this redirect also helps to validate your child's request.

WINNING IN YOUR IMAGINATION

This technique is about allowing your child's imagination to fill in the blanks for what the need really means to your child. For example, if your child wants a sleepover when it's your time with your child, and you have really been looking forward to the time together, you might say, "If you were able to have this sleepover, what were you planning to do?" Your child might share all the fun things that she was planning, and you could validate how fun that would be. You could then offer to perhaps host the sleepover at your home instead of her going somewhere else, so you still have time with your daughter and get a glimpse of her world. Or if there is a better time for the sleepover, you could say, "I would love for you to have a sleepover just like you described on a day that we can plan better for it. Let's look at the calendar to see what will work."

Winning in your imagination works even better with grade-school children who like to ask for toys and things at every store you go to. Ask your child, "If you had that toy, how would you play with it?" Listen as well as you can to your child's wondrous ideas on how he would play with the toy. Validate how fun that would be. If he continues to ask for the toy, then offer to add it on a birthday list or holiday gift list.

CHECKLISTS

Create a checklist for your kids for things they need to do and be responsible for. This technique is helpful for children ages five and older. You can use pictures when your children are little to illustrate brushing teeth, getting dressed, and picking up toys. Checklists can be fun for your children too because they can check off each thing they do and feel a sense of accomplishment. A checklist can also build routine into your child's day and teach responsibility.

For children who need redirection at stores from buying toys, use an app on your phone for making lists and have a list exclusive to your child's wishes. You can tell him, "That's a lovely toy. Let's put it on your list right now." Have your child see you type it on the list and show your child. The list helps validate your child's wish; it also validates that you really heard him. Most children will feel very pleased with putting wishes on the list.

TIME-IN

Rather than issuing a time-out, consider sitting with your child and taking a break to process what your child is feeling that is causing the misbehavior. Sitting with your child, rather than leaving her alone, also lets her know that you are there for her, even when she misbehaves. Your child may want alone time, and that's okay, but resist the notion of leaving your child alone as a way to punish the behavior.

Time-ins are also effective as a reset button because they help your child re-regulate. You can use your physicality by providing a containing hug and by whispering or speaking your request firmly but softly. For example, if your child is running in the house when you do not allow running in the house, you might catch your running child, and while firmly but gently holding her, you might say very calmly, "Running in the house right now seems like so much fun to you, and you may run outside tomorrow. Now it's time to slow our bodies down and put toys away. I will hold the toy bin, and you can place the toys into the bin."

NATURAL CONSEQUENCES

There is such value in letting your child learn through natural consequences. Remember the goal is not immediate consequence; it is ultimately to teach a lesson that corrects behavior. Correcting behavior often takes repetitive experiences, and logical and natural consequences help expedite these lessons. The more time you practice working with natural and logical consequences, the more naturally it will come. For example, your twelve-year-old daughter has a science project that you can tell she put little effort into. Rather than fixing it for her, you ask your daughter if this was her best effort, to which she responds emphatically and slightly irritated with you, "Yes. Geez, Mom, it's fine." Your daughter then takes her science project to school and shortly after comes home very sad that she received a D+. This natural consequence becomes an optimum teaching moment because she has the opportunity to learn what she needs to improve upon for presentations. As a result, she will learn how to go to her teacher and find out what she needed to work on to get a better grade. This natural consequence teaches personal responsibility, builds resilience, work ethic, and how to raise the bar higher for oneself academically.

CONTINGENCY STRATEGIES

Setting your child up for a yes as much as possible is a really effective practice. It won't fix the problem every time, but it can keep the situation from escalating, and it can give your child something to look forward to upon completion of a specific task. The parent says yes to what the child wants, provided that it is safe and within family values, but to a time when it is more convenient, or when other priorities need to get finished first. For example, your seven-year-old asks for another book after getting tucked in and reading the allotted two books for bedtime. A contingent response would sound like, "Yes, you may have more books tomorrow. In fact, if you get up and dressed on time, then we will have extra time to read a book before you go to school."

REFLECT, WRITE, AND READ

This is an effective strategy for older children (age eight and older) who are able to write and read because it causes them to reflect on their behavior and how it affected others. This is an empathy builder discipline as well because it teaches a lesson and helps the child take personal responsibility. It is also great for tweens and teens because they have to think about the consequences of their actions; a much needed impulse control skill in these tough developmental years. For example, your ten-year-old daughter Julie was caught telling another girl at school that she couldn't join her clique because her clique didn't think she was cool enough. You would respond to your daughter by saying, "You may write about cliques and how cliques make people in the clique and out of the clique feel. Also, what are you thinking and feeling about how you handled the situation at school? How do you think the other child felt, and how would you handle this situation differently in the future? When you are done, you may read it to me, and we will discuss it."

EMPOWERING YOUR CHILD'S PERSONAL RESPONSIBILITY

Having your child take ownership of the problem is a must. Asking questions is key. The one who is asking the questions is the one in power. As parents, we tell our kids what to do way too much. For example, your six-year-old son Leo took the LEGO set your eight-year-old son Jack had completed and set aside. Leo broke the set and left it behind the couch for Jack to find after the fact. You could respond by saying, "Leo, I'm confused. Jack's LEGO set was set aside on the mantle to make sure it would be safe, but somehow it landed broken behind the couch . . ." (then the parent waits until the child speaks). If Leo acknowledges, then say, "Jack feels really angry and upset. He worked hard on his LEGO plane. What do you need to do to make things better with Jack? If the mantle is too tempting for you to reach, where do you think Jack and Mom should put the finished LEGO sets?" By asking questions and waiting on the answers, your child is compelled to take responsibility and come up with solutions to problems he created. If he needs your help with solutions, then you can give choices.

SPEAKING WELL OF YOUR CHILD WHEN SHE IS IN EARSHOT

Your children thrive on knowing how you think and feel about them. Your perception of your children is the building block for their internalized concept of themselves. This concept is more easily understood in the phrase "I am what I think *you* think I am." If your child hears you saying to someone, "Little Kenny . . . he is just so aggressive with his brother." Then Kenny will continue to be more aggressive because he hears that this is what you expect of him. Since your words as a parent have such power, use your forces for good. Consider saying genuine affirming statements to others in earshot of your child that relate to behaviors you would like to see more of. For example, if you would like your child to stop yelling so much around the house, let him hear you say to your friend on the phone, "I have really noticed Johnny making such a strong effort in using his in-house voice. When he speaks respectfully to his sister, it just warms my heart as his mother to see his kindness come out." What you think of your children and say about them often becomes a self-fulfilling prophecy.

Control only what you can control with your child. You can't *make* a child fall asleep or force an infant to stop crying.

SHARE POWER

Look for opportunities to provide smaller choices where your child's opinion counts. For example, offer two choices when you can for making your children's lunch, what they would like to be for Halloween, what activity they would enjoy doing in the afternoon, which sport they would like to play in the fall, and so on. When you offer choices, then your child can feel empowered. Your child will also respect you more when you have to make a final decision on the really important decisions if you share power in the smaller more age appropriate decisions.

Specific Discipline Challenges

There are specific discipline issues that can arise in coparenting. When these issues become a problem, they have the capability of being toxic ruptures in families.

SPANKING

The discipline practice of spanking is one of those challenges that can have adverse effects on the parent-child relationship and your child's self-esteem. Deciding to spank a child can have long-lasting effects in a child's mind. Conscious coparents refrain from spanking or hitting their children as a discipline practice because having a connected relationship comes first. You want to avoid any kind of threatening punishment that's aggressive, humiliating, or inflicts pain. Often parents spank because they feel powerless in the moment. Punitive punishments can and will affect the child's attachment to the parent. When spanked, the child's brain interprets pain as a threat, and the neural circuitry connections die in the brain as a result. It is the same part of the brain that mediates physical pain and processes social rejection, so the child's brain is wiring social rejection and pain in combination with spanking.

Spanking also teaches the child that the parent had no other solution but to inflict bodily pain. If children learn best from modeling, then when a parent spanks as the main disciplinary practice, the child is learning that aggressiveness is the only way to solve conflict. Spanking also stops misbehavior momentarily, which is mostly why parents use spanking, but it can also foster the ability to conceal misbehavior. Resist spanking your child out of anger because the message you are sending becomes more about how angry you are than what the child actually did to deserve the spanking.

A recent study out of Southern Methodist University followed children who had misbehaved and received spankings as their punishment. Astonishingly, the children who were spanked went right back to their same misbehavior in just seven minutes.

If you have a coparent who uses corporal punishment as a form of discipline, do your best to have a thorough understanding of when your coparent uses spanking or hitting as a punishment. As a coparent, you have the right to ask about your coparent's discipline practice. Coparents who ignore, verbally abuse, or attempt to bully their coparent may also bully in their parenting. In addition, if your coparent leaves a mark on your child after punishing, this is considered child abuse and is reportable to your local child protective services. Look for signs from your children of withdrawal, not wanting to see their other parent, frequent sickness, stomachaches, headaches, or trouble sleeping.

STEPPARENTS AND LIVE-IN RELATIONSHIPS

In conscious coparenting, building a support network that loves your children is highly desirable. You want to spend time with people who respect that you are a parent, and that your children have a coparent who they love very much and spend time with. When stepparents or live-in relationships come into the picture, you must set clear boundaries about how the stepparent can discipline. As the coparent, you are the primary guardian during your shared time with your child, and you should be the only one who disciplines. This is particularly true for live-in relationships. A new boyfriend or girlfriend should not have the authority to discipline your child because they haven't built a relationship with the child. If your child does not want to spend time with your new relationship, pay attention and try to find out why. Your child may be trying to tell you something very important about how your new relationship is making them feel.

Think about a recent challenge you had in the area of discipline with your child. Think about how you and your coparent were able to work together effectively, or not effectively. Reflect on how you handled it, how it worked, and brainstorm other possibilities.

Stepparents need to foster a trusting relationship with the child. If you want your child to have a thriving relationship, then let them find positive memories to build on rather than having your new spouse discipline. Remember, you are the primary parent, and a stepparent plays a secondary role in the raising of your child. A stepparent should never be the primary disciplinarian of your child. It actually takes half the amount of years of a child's age for a stepparent to foster a secure attachment with your child. So if your child is four years old, then it will take two years. If a child is age ten, then it will take five years of bonding for the child and stepparent to feel securely attached.

Important Points to Consider

Coparenting has its share of issues specific to discipline. Discipline goes better if you both can be on the same page with positive discipline techniques. Here are a few areas to think about with discipline:

O Discuss discipline techniques with your coparent and find where you agree and how you might both handle the situation so your child is getting the most similar message as possible.

O Discipline can often be construed as punishment, and when a parent is focused on punishing her child, the lesson is lost. Remember you want to use parenting practices that teach and foster ongoing connection in the parenting relationship.

O Stepparents and long-term relationships are secondary caregivers and not primary disciplinarians. Specifically discuss with your significant other how you would like to address discipline issues in your home.

O Spanking is not a solution for teaching your child to behave. Many options will set limits and keep your child's self-esteem intact.

 **CHAPTER 13**

Repairing Coparenting Ruptures

Parenting is fraught with handling ruptures in your relationship, whether big or small. If you are coparenting because of a divorce or breakup, your child experienced a rupture in the changing of her home environment and her parents no longer being together. Children handle the loss of their intact family differently based on their age and circumstances. Typically, there is some semblance of grieving that needs to take place in order for the child to make sense of the loss. Part of a child's grieving may be feeling angry, sad, or frustrated with his parents because they are no longer together. Ruptures occur when a child has an emotional disconnection from a parent.

Types of Ruptures

Ruptures happen just about every day. There are certain kinds of ruptures that can happen daily in parenting, and larger ruptures can have lasting impact on the psyche. In Dr. Dan Siegel and Mary Hartzell's book *Parenting from the Inside Out*, the authors explain the four kinds of ruptures that can occur relationally. Let's look at the types of ruptures coparents can encounter.

THE OSCILLATING RUPTURE

The first is an oscillating rupture, which is when a parent and child are not attuning because one individual wants connection and the other individual wants solitude. A good example is when a child is playing on his own and is very content with his alone time, and then the parent notices and interrupts the play because the parent wants to engage. The same is true when a parent is on the computer getting the to-do list done, and the child comes in the room and just starts a conversation, or ignores that the parent is busy and tries to grab her attention. Both examples are experiences where one individual is not attuning to the different state that the other is in. Oscillating ruptures are the most common parenting ruptures, and they are likely to happen when parenting alone with multiple children.

To be mindful of preventing an oscillating rupture with your child, tell him gently that you need alone time and you will be able to play shortly after you are done with your project. If your child wants to show you something he is very excited about, then, if at all possible, give him your complete attention for that minute and then go back to what you are doing. You don't want your child to take it personally or begin to think that you don't want to spend time with him. In coparenting, you can reduce oscillating ruptures by staying as present as possible during your shared time. Be willing to put your phone or tablet down and give your child your undivided attention as much as you can.

BENIGN RUPTURES

We all have moments when we don't understand what our child is trying to tell us. The technical term for this communication mismatching is a benign rupture. Benign ruptures occur when a parent does not understand the messages her child is sending because the parent is preoccupied or lacks understanding about what the message being communicated means. If a child has a developmental speech delay it can also cause benign ruptures. When a child cognitively knows what he is trying to communicate but is misunderstood because his verbal mechanics are not functioning properly, he can feel painfully frustrated.

Benign ruptures in coparenting households may manifest if you aren't aware of what your child is sharing because the event happened during his shared time with his other parent. If you are grasping that your child is excited about what he is sharing, but you are having a hard time following the full meaning of the story, first attune to his feeling state of what he is sharing. You might say something like, "I can tell you are very excited about what happened. Tell me more."

Feeling preoccupied in the initial stage of coparenting is very common because many coparents are transitioning into a significant life change. With major life changes, it is easy to think about your problems and hard to shut off the emotional chatter. The problem happens when your child doesn't feel or sense that he has your full focus as he is trying to share something with you. Be mindful of how preoccupied you are during your time with your child and set a strong intention to remain present as much as possible. Benign ruptures happen daily with your child, but if a child is in a heightened emotional state, a benign rupture with you can feel painful, especially if he is not understood.

LIMIT-SETTING RUPTURE

Kids need to have limits. They also need to understand that moms and dads have expectations around behavior, and it is important to clearly define what constitutes misbehavior. Although setting limits is a necessity when parenting, it can also cause a disconnect between parent and child. Limit-setting ruptures happen when a parent is not attuning to why her child is misbehaving in the first place and then disciplines the child. Limit-setting ruptures also happen when the child doesn't like the limit set by the parent, and it causes distress. The key to staying in connection during these limit-setting interactions is to attune to your child's primary emotional state. You attune through engaging your child empathically and compassionately.

When empathy doesn't work, and your child is still distressed, it's important not to bend your limit or punish your child more for feeling distressed. Offer a message that you understand that your child doesn't like the limit set and it's okay that he feels angry. At these times, it's appropriate to let him sit in his pain and figure it out himself.

Coparenting issues may arise with limit-setting ruptures if you discipline differently than your coparent does. It can be confusing for a child to have one set of rules and expectations in one home and a different set of rules and expectations in another home. Kids typically do not like to hear a limit being set in the moment, but in the long run, children feel a sense of safety when they have parents who set limits. This safety might not be acknowledged by your child because he is mad that he is not getting what he wanted. This is to be expected. However, your child will be able to acknowledge the positives in the limits set in the long term. Do your best to discuss setting limits as coparents, so your child receives similar messages in both homes. This way your child will know that his parents will handle expectations similarly, and both parents are aligned on this message.

TOXIC RUPTURES

Toxic ruptures are the most difficult ruptures of all because they involve intense emotional distress and a despairing disconnection between a parent and a child, which is harmful to a child's sense of self. Toxic ruptures happen when a parent is coming from a dysregulated state and behaves from pure emotion without thinking through how her actions might harm the child. The child then feels dysregulated by the experience with his parent, and over time, if the toxic rupture continues, a break in the attachment with the parent will occur. In order to stop the toxic rupture from continuing, the parent must emotionally regulate herself and consciously choose to disconnect from the toxic interaction with her child. Toxic ruptures have to be repaired with children in an empathic, effective, and timely manner, so the child's self-esteem and sense of self is not damaged by the experience.

Coparents who may have experienced ruptures in the past with their child need to make time for repairing them with their child. The heart of a toxic rupture for parent and child is actually shame. Shame, simply put, is a message that says, "I am bad." If you have been handling situations with a child with a sense of shame, where you are giving yourself this message, or you are translating this message to your child in your interaction with each other, then take the time to process your feelings of shame. If you find yourself inherently feeling that you are bad, it usually comes from an early experience in your childhood narrative that was shame based. Shame causes the parent to be overly concerned with what others might think, which makes it difficult to attend to the child's signal.

> Shame makes it difficult for you to attune to your child because early shame messages can preoccupy your thinking and feeling processes. You can change the shame legacy by understanding yourself better and taking the steps to heal.

SIGNS OF A RUPTURE WITH YOUR CHILD

You can tell that a rupture has impacted your child when you see signs of extreme routine withdrawal, aggressive reactions on the part of the child, or major changes in sleep and eating habits. The subtle signs children will present after a rupture are avoiding eye contact, pretending not to hear or understand you, avoiding conversation, and a shift in voice quality.

If you have acknowledged that you hurt your child's feelings and your child cannot remain open to your apology, this means that your child is still hurt, and you probably need to spend more time understanding what it was like for your child to experience that rupture with you.

Whenever possible, coparents who have ruptures should ideally repair any ruptures during their time with the child. If the rupture was significant enough that your child cannot repair it with you because the hurt was too great, then honor your child's hurt by giving him time to heal. It can feel intrusive to a child to have a parent who is anxious about repairing and pushing for repair when the child is not ready. Toxic rupture repairs can take time because parents have to rebuild trust. Divorce can feel like a toxic rupture for your child because you are changing what your child knows to be family. Helping your child understand that both parents will continue to be available to him, even though he is living in two different homes, will take time to prove to him because the actions of the parents have to convince the child that he can trust this arrangement.

Conscious Coparents Repair

Repairing a rupture with your child is more important than attuning to your child. Repairing a rupture means that the parent acknowledges that the child was impacted emotionally by a distressing interaction with the parent. Repairing is the opportunity to make sense of the disconnection between you and your child. It is crucial that if you have a rupture with your child, you understand how your behavior may have contributed to the rupture in order to initiate the repair process. Failing to repair a rupture can lead to a deepening sense of disconnection between parent and child. Over time, this can lead to greater emotional distance.

Research shows that repairing a rupture with your child is more important than attuning to your child. The reason is that repairing with a child acts as validation that your child experienced something hurtful. Acknowledging the hurt helps your child let it go and forgive. When you repair, you are also modeling how to ask for forgiveness.

Coparents who need to repair with their child have to get centered and calm before any kind of repair can take place. This is because you need to return to a regulated state; your heart rate is level, the intensity of your voice has reduced, your eye gaze is soft, and you can think rationally and have a better understanding of why you behaved the way you did, either with your child or in front of your child. Repair initiates the process of reconnection with your child. Since your child may have experienced shame from the experience, you need to be the one to initiate repair.

You don't want to "just forget" a rupture with your child. Remember, timely intervention is key.

MANAGING EMOTIONS

Productive repair work requires you to have a solid understanding in what you were feeling and thinking at the time you experienced a rupture with your child. You may need to journal or practice some self-soothing techniques in order to feel more available to repair. Your own emotional discomfort about the repairs needs to have subsided before you can sit with your child and process what happened. Your child should not have to feel responsible for making you feel better about what happened. Signs that your child may be feeling responsible for your feelings are: your child trying to cheer you up, asking you frequently if you are mad at her, excessively clingy, or talking to you about your relationship with your coparent more as a friend than your child. These signs represent your child feeling anxious about their relationship with you and needing to feel more secure.

Practice a guided imagery exercise where you see an image of the rupture in your mind, and then hold the word *compassion* in bold letters in front of the image to help you associate compassion with instances you are not proud of. The more you practice being compassionate with yourself, the more you will be able to be compassionate with others. Everyone needs kindness, including you. Modeling compassion to your child will help her learn how to be self-compassionate and create a reparative mindset for the long run.

Some children who get caught in managing their parent's emotions experience being a parentified child. A parentified child is one who is seen more as a peer to their parent and is given responsibilities beyond what is age appropriate. These responsibilities can vary from managing a home, other siblings, as well as their parent's emotions. Do your best to assure your child that she is not responsible for you and how you feel. Demonstrate to your child that you can handle your feelings. Focus on how your child is feeling and review with her the facts of how you both created the rupture, and how you want to repair it, so nobody has to continue to feel bad about what happened.

If you have a history where your own parents did not repair ruptures, then repairing a rupture may be difficult for you. Take the time to make sense of how the lack of repair may have impacted your history so you can be more conscious of how to repair in a healthy way with your child.

If you find you are upset at yourself more than at your child for how you handled things, notice any judgments you are making about yourself. Judgment statements are usually harsh critical statements that tear you down rather than support your growth. Coparenting can often draw out more judgments because you are concerned about what others are thinking of your parenting since you are parenting in two different homes. You may experience more pressure, feel as if you have to be perfect, and feel like you can't make mistakes. Practice being "lovingly curious," which means reflecting on your thoughts with a sympathetic sense of wonder. When you are lovingly curious, you invite more compassion into your self-reflection rather than condemnation. Once you have figured out what triggered you and have grounded yourself after the rupture, you can think of a plan for handling the situation differently next time. If possible, you might also think about what might be a preventative plan. This is also a good tool to talk through with your child if there is a tendency to provoke one another into ruptures.

Discuss how you can come up with a plan together before things get heightened; taking a break from the conversation is often an important step.

PARENTS INITIATE REPAIR

Parents must be the initiator of repair, not the child. Even if your child behaved very poorly and embarrassed or angered you, conscious coparents initiate repair with their children. The reason is you are the adult, and your child typically does not have the same capacity to handle conflict. Parents who do not go to their children to repair are prolonging the disconnection. Some parents expect their child to come to them first to repair, but consider what this behavior exemplifies. In a conscious parenting relationship, modeling to your child how to repair gives your child an internal modeling of how to forgive and move toward closure. Some circumstances require many conversations of repair, but what helps is being the kind of parent who is available for repair and presents in a nondefensive manner.

You may feel ashamed of how you handled certain issues during your divorce or as a coparent, but it's never too late to repair. In an age appropriate way, take the time to acknowledge to your child if you mishandled a situation or caused unnecessary hurt for him. Check in with him if there is residual pain that you need to address from the divorce.

Reflect back to your childhood on how your parents handled apologizing or repairing with you when one of them mishandled a situation. Think of a time growing up when you may have experienced a limit-setting rupture and a toxic rupture. Consider how it made you feel. If your parents had a toxic rupture with you, reflect on if they repaired the rupture. If your parent didn't repair the rupture, how have you made sense of it now?

STEPS TOWARD REPAIR

There are a few steps to help you regain centeredness. Consider the following:

- Gain perspective on the interaction by creating mental and sometimes physical distance.

- Begin with deep breathing to calm your nervous system.

- Use coping skills that help you alleviate stress, like exercise, mindfulness meditation practices, focused attention exercises, and prayer.

- Reflect on what conflict triggers led to having a rupture.

- Continue to hold the awareness you have about how you handled the rupture, and at the same time, create space within yourself to be there for your child's experience of the rupture.

- Acknowledge your behavior and think about how it might have been scary or distressing to your child.

- Normalize that even parents can have meltdowns or tantrums.

- Bringing closure with the rupture is different depending on the child's age.

- Helping your kids make sense of the rupture helps to re-regulate their nervous systems, and it helps their brains make sense of what happened.

Acknowledge That Trust May Need to Be Re-earned

When children have relied on the safety and security of their intact family and a separation or divorce occurs, it is normal for them not to feel as secure. A child looks at the world from the perspective of "my world is an extension of me." This perspective remains and gradually dissipates as the child matures in his grade-school years. When a child sees his parents divorcing, or living in two different homes, there may an initial distrust about how coparenting is going to work, and how it will impact his relationship with each of his parents. When you begin coparenting it takes time to create an effective structure together for your family. Acknowledge to your child that you love him so very much, and there might be awkward moments initially where Mom and Dad are figuring out how to best work together. If your child witnessed past fights between coparents, this may also contribute to his discomfort with the situation. Attuning to your child's discomfort, really listening to how he is feeling, and listening to any fears he may have about the coparenting arrangement is important to address.

COMMON FEARS

Children in coparenting homes may have certain fears that arise in a coparenting arrangement. The first fear is not seeing the other parent regularly. Children who get to see a parent every other weekend may feel sad, confused, or think their parent doesn't love them enough to see them more. Explain to your children why the coparenting arrangement selected for them will help. Let your children know that coparenting is the choice that works best for the parents, and it will not take away from the love and care that both parents want to provide for them.

Some children who have long-standing powerful memories of their families together may continue to wish that their parents could work it out and parent them under the same roof. It's similar to the Disney/Pixar movie *Inside Out* where the main character, Riley, has core memories of both parents supporting her that bring her joy or comfort. These memories are rich in feeling secure and loved by both parents. It is normal for children to want to build similar memories with both parents, and you can continue to build on those memories of comfort for your child. Coparents who put the comfort of their children first can both be available at the very beginning of the coparenting relationship. Comfort can still look like both parents sitting down with their child to have important conversations and provide loving and caring gestures. Your children will adapt to the change in the living arrangement, but do your best in working with your coparent to provide the emotional support they need. The fantasy of parents still living together may subside, providing the child continually feels supported by both parents. Having comforting experiences, where the coparents are present for the child, can have lasting positive effects.

BE WARY OF BEING TOO DISMISSIVE OR TOO INTRUSIVE

When it comes to repairing with your children, being careful to attune to your child's feelings about the rupture is essential for it to heal between parent and child. Making statements like "Don't feel that way," or "Why are you making such a big deal out of this," or "I already said I'm sorry, what more do you want from me" are dismissive statements that tell your child that he is not allowed to feel the way he does. Dismissive language and statements can often be a defense for parents for a couple of reasons.

First, dismissing your child's pain helps you not to feel what it was really like for your child. It may make you feel anxious that your child hurts from an encounter between the two of you. That is a painful thought for any parent. Second, you may not want to take responsibility for your part in the rupture. It's not easy to look at your own behavior with your child. However, when you have the emotional availability to listen really well to what your child felt during the rupture, you are letting him know that his feelings matter to you and that you can handle how he feels. Negative messages that grown-ups struggle with, like" I'm too needy" or "I'm a burden," are greatly reduced for children who have parents who are available to listen and attune to their hurt. As a result, the children will heal and become more resilient.

Being too intrusive with a repair is the other side of the extreme where the parent's anxiety about the rupture takes over the ability to repair for the child. It actually becomes more about the parent's feelings than the child's feelings. Parents who have a tendency to over attune may frequently bring up the rupture to check in with the child, or bring it up at inopportune times where it takes the child off guard, or bring it up when the child is not in the right frame of mind to process. Often, parents may also insert adult reasoning, or excuses for the parent, into the intrusive repairing. As a result, the repair doesn't fully happen, and it becomes more of a rupture in the parent-child relationship. Repairing right away is a good idea, but you also have to sense that your child is available and ready to repair.

Sometimes waiting a day and letting your grade-school child know that you want to talk about this further, when he is ready, is a better approach. When dealing with young children, going to your child immediately after and saying sorry for how you behaved, and processing any sad, angry, confused, or scared feelings your child may have from the encounter, is usually the best approach. Once the repair has happened and your child seems more relaxed and feels understood, then let it be, unless your child brings it up. Typically, when a child continues to bring up a rupture, it's because he hasn't fully made sense of it yet.

Repairing Ruptures with Your Coparent

The majority of coparents have extensive histories together, and for many, there are more hurtful memories than positive ones. When you begin the healing process for yourself, you are choosing to repair for you, not necessarily your coparent. Forgiveness is a process. It's the process of letting go. You deserve the ability to let the hurt go. Forgiveness can feel a little terrifying if you have held onto resentments for a long time. These resentments are like heavy rocks in a backpack you are trying to carry uphill. Resentment is seductive because it cons you into thinking you need to keep holding onto the pain so you won't allow yourself to be hurt this badly again. Resentment also may speak to your identity. If you see yourself as a wronged person, and you continue to retell the story of your divorce or separation from this perspective, then letting go of resentments may feel like letting go of a part of who you are. But the things you have been through do not define who you are. It is how you handle the issues that define who you are.

If you are holding onto past resentments with your coparent, ask yourself how that is helping you personally, or as a coparent.

Feeling stuck in old entrenched patterns with your coparent can continue to surface throughout the coparenting relationship. This can become particularly difficult if you have extensive negative history with one another where unfair fighting practices take place. Recognizing how disagreements with your coparent trigger early experiences is the best way to clean this up emotionally for yourself. In order to consciously live as a conscious self, you have to allow that self to expand. Part of growing into one's whole self as a conscious coparent is being intentional about identifying how your early childhood issues get re-triggered. Comprehending your personal triggers in your coparenting will help you to be more present and free from the residual hurt in the future because you will reduce personalizing behavior. Remember, it's not about the behavior. It is about how you perceive the behavior. Processing your own issues, and what you bring to your coparenting relationship, is a sign of self-respect.

As Eleanor Roosevelt once said, "No one can make you feel inferior without your consent."

Everyone has relational triggers and you can't avoid them. Understanding your own feeling landscape, and the hot spots that are underlying those triggers, will help reduce your reactivity with your coparent. Certain relationships bring out similar feelings, and often there are common themes for individuals that will manifest in all aspects of life. For example, if you relate to feeling disrespected, you probably have had experiences where you have felt disrespected in the workplace, in friendships, in an intimate relationship, and with your kids. Changing your paradigm about triggers can also be helpful in releasing resentments. Rather than holding onto the hurt, see an issue that you have with your coparent as a personal opportunity for growth and healing. It's a conscious paradigm shift in how you view life issues.

STEPS TO REGAIN SELF-CONTROL

Repercussions from a fall-out with your coparent can have lasting effects. Being able to take care of your emotions quickly after a rupture will help you think proactively about the issues. Follow these steps when you need to self-soothe and regain composure after a rupture with your coparent:

1. **Acknowledge to yourself that you are triggered.** The simple act of acknowledgment can be enough to help you walk away and start working on the issue for yourself, rather than going on the attack.

2. **In the middle of a coparenting conflict, politely table the conversation for later.** You don't have to have all the answers. If you need time to process, then schedule a time to discuss the issue further after you have had time to think.

3. **Contemplate your part in the interaction, and contemplate what the trigger was away from the event.** This helps you access your higher mode of processing that is found in the left hemisphere of your brain. Upon accessing the left hemisphere, you can integrate self-reflection, attunement, and empathy into how you repair. There can be a high degree of vulnerability after having a rupture, and that is normal. Do your best to be compassionate with yourself; know that vulnerability can be helpful tool, rather than a negative.

4. **Breathe deeply.** Breath work that has a shorter inhalation and a longer exhalation works best to help calm.

5. **Journal or talk to someone you trust.** Take the time to journal or talk to a friend whom you respect about parenting. Make sure you have a friend who doesn't continue to fuel your anger by bad-mouthing your coparent. Share your upset. Receive counsel if you have a repetitive pattern of getting triggered by the same issue and you can't seem to stop. Use your journal to understand your "hot buttons" so you can track patterns in order to work on them.

6. **Sit down or move your body if you need to release pent-up energy.** Sometimes sitting too long when upset, or for others moving too much, causes more upset. Help your body self-regulate by adjusting as necessary.

7. **Use regulation strategies to help calm down.** Counting backward from ten helps engage the left hemisphere (the logical side) of the brain when the right hemisphere (the emotional side) of the brain is flooded. Work to stay in the moment while re-regulatory calming strategies take hold. This can usually take a minimum of fifteen to sixty minutes.

8. **Once you feel re-regulated, take the steps to repair with your co-parent as needed.** When repairing, reflect on the reactivity you experienced and consider how your threshold has expanded, or your resilience has increased. Your resiliency will be like a muscle that helps you manage other future coparenting situations.

Case Study: Marta and Caleb

Marta and Caleb had been married for ten years and had three children, seven-year-old Ian, five-year-old Rosie, and three-year-old Jesse. It was a busy life in their household with three children, and both Marta and Caleb had busy careers. Until one day when Caleb left his work computer on and Marta went to check something online, only to find an open e-mail from a female escort Caleb was planning to see on his next work trip. As she looked closer, Marta discovered several e-mails to other escorts over the course of the last three years. Everything she thought she knew to be true in her relationship felt like a complete lie. Marta confronted Caleb, and he confessed. Marta divorced Caleb shortly after. What hurt the most for Marta was not how Caleb had betrayed their vows or even put her own sexual health at risk; it was the fact that she had signed up to be married for her whole life to one person, and now she no longer had this legacy to offer to her children. When she looked in her children's eyes, and particularly her littlest one, she deeply grieved for them because she never wanted them to come from a divorced home. She was so angry with Caleb.

In their coparenting, her pain was so great that she could barely speak to him. She set up pickups and drop-offs at school so they never had to see each other, and she had Caleb wait outside if pickups happened at her house. All the interaction typically occurred through brief e-mails. The children didn't talk about their father around their mom because they sensed her hurt, and it felt confusing and awkward to bring him up.

Two years into their coparenting, Marta recognized that she continued to feel resentful, and it was having adverse effects on her kids. Her middle child, Rosie, did not want to leave her mom alone, which at first Marta thought was just because Rosie preferred her to Caleb. In reality, Rosie was internalizing Marta's anxiety, and Rosie didn't feel like she could leave Marta alone. Marta realized that her resentments were causing her more harm than good.

Marta went into therapy to process her divorce, and through much effort she reached a point of acceptance, feeling emotionally lighter after a year of therapy. She learned that forgiveness was a process of letting go for herself, and she didn't want to become bitter. It took some time, but she was thankful she took the initiative to do the emotional work necessary because of how it enhanced her relationship with her children. As a result, she didn't personalize how Caleb had behaved in their marriage, and she recognized she needed a better working relationship with him for the kids to feel safer in their coparenting. She began to check in with him at pickup, and she asked him to join her for parent conferences at school. Their oldest, Ian, joined a select soccer team. Marta was able to sit with the kids, and Caleb was able to cheer Ian on. It took time for Marta, but she was finally in a place to make her coparenting work.

Important Points to Consider

Over time, relational ruptures can cause great distance. Coparents who are willing to work together to help their child work through residual hurts from divorce, or loss of their family no longer living under the same roof, should think about the following:

O Ruptures happen all the time. The difference is if you take the time to acknowledge the rupture, then it will keep your child from feeling misunderstood or holding onto old hurts.

O Repair is more important than attuning in relationships. Coparents need to acknowledge if the divorce or separation has impacted their kids.

○ If you have ruptures from your previous relationship with your coparent, take the time to make sense of it, so you don't have to be burdened by the hurt.

○ Soothe yourself when triggered, so you don't act impulsively and add more fuel to the fire.

 **CHAPTER 14**

How Present Are You?

Coparenting can have its share of challenges. Even if you have previously outlined in your coparenting agreement how you plan to work together, you won't have covered every issue. Little exchanges sometimes build up over time and can cause some bigger challenges for coparents. Part of your process as a conscious coparent is learning to be mindful in your parenting. Coparents who have more full-time custody arrangements may have less downtime to care for their own needs. If you live a fast-paced life, have multiple children, and/or a demanding job, it can grow increasingly difficult to stay present and be self-aware. Part of living consciously is the ability to self-observe how present you really are.

Practice Self-Awareness with Quality Time

Conscious coparenting is about making the most of your time with your children. Making the most of your time means choosing to be as present as possible when you are with your children. Some parents think that making the most of their time means staying incredibly busy and running their children to different enrichment classes and sports. Remember, it's the amount of time you spend and how you spend it that matters most.

Quality time is actually the combination of both quality and how much time you are spending with your child. When you reflect on the rhythm of your household, making sure you have connective time with your child is a must. The quality of the time needs to be relational, where you and your child are feeling connected in being together. For many families, electronics like TV, video games, music, and the Internet have become substitutes for the relationship. The downside to this is that families become more isolated and less relational, even around family entertainment. Things can never replace a connective relationship. When a person feels truly connected to another and has the experience of being seen and heard, it is irreplaceable. If you find yourself substituting things for your time, then acknowledge it and make the necessary changes. When you have time with your child, focus on the relationship.

Choosing a few activities with your kids where spending money is not a part of the time spent with one another is a helpful tool because you'll have a go-to list if you are wondering what to do next. Outings where you are relating with one another, like going on a nature walk or playing together in the park, are great ways to get in quality time. For older children, taking them to see athletic events in a sport they love can be a special bonding moment. There are special enrichment outings, like going to museums or seeing a cultural event, that enhance your child's learning. Routine additions to the schedule, such as volunteering, Boy Scouts, Girl Scouts, or a regular library day, are activities that create consistency in your home's routine and offer quality time with each other. Structured organizations, like scouting, also build confidence, a new skillset, and provide opportunities for parents to get involved.

CHOOSING OUTINGS ONLY FOR QUALITY TIME

Some coparents find themselves taking their children out for frequent outings and activities during their shared time as a way to spend time with their children. Typically, coparents who have less time with their children may find themselves going on outings that are high in entertainment value. This may be for a host of reasons, such as:

○ Just wanting to have fun with your kids, and knowing your kids love amusement parks, fun zones, movies, video games.

○ You feel guilty that you don't see your children as regularly as you would ideally like because of your work schedule or other factors.

○ It's actually really hard to relax at home with the kids because you don't know what to do with the time. You have a tendency to like distractions.

○ You're worried your child will get bored and won't want to spend time with you.

High entertainment activities are not inherently bad, but you may want to ask yourself if you have a tendency to use your shared time with the kids with frequent entertainment outings. "What is my intention?" Do you feel guilty about anything in your coparenting, and are you trying to compensate?

Entertaining your children may be a form of distraction because you want the time to be fun and enjoyable for both parent and child. Perhaps the deeper meaning behind distracting you and your kids during your shared time is that you may be sitting with some painful feelings about the changes that have occurred in your family. If you take the time to slow down and just be with each other without all the activities, what might you discover about your relationship with your children? Many parents have the misconception that the more fun they have, the better memories their children will have about their childhoods. Often, fun for children is not about how many times Dad or Mom took them to Disneyland. Fun is about how present Mom or Dad was with the child in the small things like a board game, active reading together, or sharing some laughs during a car ride.

Conscious Play with Your Child

An aspect of quality time with children is the parent's ability to be present and play. The significance of conscious play cannot be underestimated because play is being in the moment with your child and following her lead. Play can be very empowering for your child when you allow her to be in charge of the ideas of play and the storylines, rather than inserting your own ideas. Following your child's lead in play demonstrates respecting your child's imaginative process. A recent research study on play showed that children play approximately eight hours less per week than they did ten years ago. This is because so much of children's play has become structured classes or enrichment, where a child is learning a new skill or practicing a sport in an organized setting.

For coparents who share time, setting aside time to play what their children enjoy playing is an ideal way to transition back into time together. Play also helps your child's regulatory system handle stress and builds her ability to be more resilient. This is because children use play to process how they are feeling, which results in a strengthening of your child's emotional, cognitive, social, and physical development. Playtime is also a time for your child to learn, not a time for you to teach your child something. Teaching is inadvertently happening because you are modeling that your child is worthwhile and lovable enough to receive your full attention. Imaginative play also teaches your child to practice problem solving using the character situations that she makes up. Observe how your child develops storylines for characters and notice certain themes in your child's play. Being available for twenty to thirty minutes of imaginative play, where your child leads the play, can truly rebuild connections and foster a stronger relationship with your child.

Parents play differently, depending on how their parents allowed and encouraged them to play as children. Some parents want to play board games or follow certain rules of play. Make sure to balance this kind of organized play with imaginative play. Parents also play differently depending on how much time and brain power they have left after their eight- to twelve-hour day or night job. Play does not have to be physical, but it certainly must be active and engaged.

If playing with your child is a struggle, and you find your mind wandering off and you're thinking about work or getting tired, set the intention to play for just ten minutes and to be completely present in the play with your child. Then build up with five-minute increments to a max of thirty minutes. If you have the ability to go longer, then do so. The goal is to be present, so start with a reasonable expectation.

First, model respectful behavior by setting aside all cell phones. This doesn't mean putting the phone in your pocket on vibrate, because there will be a call or text that will prompt you to say, "Wait, I need to take this." Set aside notions of how your child "should" be playing. Join without prejudice or opinions. Resist the temptation to insert drill-down questions about what they did yesterday and what they have planned for tomorrow. Let them *be* and observe. That means practice conscious listening, which is perhaps the most underused parental skill.

Improvisation games are great for a child's brain development, confidence, and social skills. Try a game called "day in the life," where you act out your entire day in pantomime as your child narrates your actions. Then switch roles.

The clock on the wall does not measure quality time. Generally, conscious play is most effective in ten- to twenty-minute blocks, then step away so you can wipe the brain slates (yours and your child's) clean and reboot. If this sounds paradoxical—*Don't count the minutes but minutes count*—it is. Ten to twenty minutes of active listening, un-judged interaction, and laughing is better than an hour of passive disengagement.

STORYTELLING

Oral storytelling is a playful art that our generation of children can often miss out on because of advancements in technologies. Storytelling fosters the child's imagination to visualize rather than watching a screen tell the story. You can be a master storyteller by using these elements of traditional folktales:

O Insert yourself, the parent, as the hero in the story (but not as a parent or wise man).

O Place yourself in a strange or alternate world.

O Include a foe or foil.

O Frame a right-or-wrong lesson within the action of the story.

O Always return home safely.

Do not include your children in the story because it will be too difficult for them to suspend their disbelief and track the plot. Oral storytelling can create a lifelong bond, teach a moral lesson without being didactic, and comfort a young person's soul.

Conscious play with your child is organic and creates a rich humanistic parent-child bonding that gives your child context for cognitive growth, while advancing language skills, building self-esteem, and creating well-adjusted young people who become happy, healthy adults.

Response Flexibility

Response flexibility in parenting terms is the parent's ability to decide how to manage one's feelings and thoughts when handling one's child. Researcher and neuroscientist Dr. Allan Schore wrote, "A person who most people would agree is delightful to be around has an optimal arousal . . . being full of life and warmth." Optimal arousal is the way a person is, and his response to other people can be spoiled by being inappropriately overaroused or underaroused to the situation. When an individual is over-aroused, this means getting anxious or angry over things that most people handle well. Underarousal means the kind of emotional flatness that makes a person seem rather dull or boring. Everyone has an optimal window of arousal where the brain's social engagement system and learning ability is working at it's ideal levels. This optimal arousal presents as the ability to stay focused and learn something new, feel engaged with the material, feel connected, and have an empathetic conversation with someone when there is a mutual sense of feeling understood.

With babies and toddlers, rocking, touch, holding, swaddling, and regulation of temperature are all part of building your child's regulatory system that needs support. These soothing exercises help your child's nervous system move back to equilibrium. Your child learns "I can get dysregulated and then I can calm down."

As conscious coparents, parenting from your window of optimal arousal provides your children with the gift of feeling fully present and relationally engaged with you on different levels. When an individual is overaroused or underaroused, it puts the individual in a state of rigidity or chaos. In rigid or chaotic states, you are not able to attune well because your own state is intruding upon your ability to be present.

Learning how to maintain longer lengths of time in optimal arousal happens when individuals take adequate care of their physical and emotional health, have a sense of purpose in their lives, and have the ability to be a secure connector in relationships. Mindfulness techniques, or focused attention exercises, are also helpful tools in building optimal arousal functioning. The ability to observe how you are feeling in your body, and disciplining your mind to follow your breath, helps to keep you grounded.

COPARENTING BOUNDARIES

Part of response flexibility is also the ability to say no to people or situations when you are at your limit. Identifying your own limits may feel hard, particularly in coparenting. This may be because you don't want your child to feel that he is not getting everything another child might from an intact family. This kind of decision-making may be inspired by parent guilt, and you would be better off allowing yourself to stay in the present and consciously decide what is in the best interests of your child, and what you can actually handle.

If you have a coparent who has requests that you feel compromise your boundaries, then think about the kind of boundaries you may need to implement. Learning how to say "no" to others can be difficult for certain people. Many coparents report feeling guilty and resentful of their coparent when he or she does not follow through on certain responsibilities and expects the other coparent to just handle it for their child. The guilt is that you love your child deeply, but you also have a coparent who is shirking responsibility, and that has a negative impact on you and your child. Coparents in this position often just pick up the slack for their coparent because it is easier to leave them feeling taken advantage of and resentful.

If you find yourself having difficulty with saying no, then holding a boundary actually teaches resiliency to your coparent. This resiliency is formed because your coparent has to think through her predicament and figure out a solution rather than over rely on your constant availability. Your coparent might find that she is capable of creating a support network of her own, which every parent needs. Another consequence would be that it also takes away the energy you need when you have your shared time and don't want to compromise your ability to be present with your own family at home. There are, of course, special circumstances that may require you to stretch and provide help more than usual, and you know what circumstances would compel you to be of more assistance. The difference is you feel like you have a choice, and you are not making the decision out of guilt.

If you have a coparent who has requests that you feel compromise your boundaries, then think about the kind of boundaries you may need to set. Learn how to say "no" to others when it compromises your ability to be present with your own family at home.

Being conscious of what your child may need from you, or from your coparent, at different stages is another area where being flexible with your responses is helpful. Don't take it personally if your child feels closer to your coparent. Closeness with one parent can happen at different stages because of similar interests, being the same gender, being the opposite gender, and similar personalities. You will still need to have your time with your child, but if your coparent has a skillset for homework that you don't, then being flexible with the schedule only benefits your child.

Case Study: Mark

Mark and Carrie had two children, a boy and a girl, ages eight and eleven respectively. They had a joint custody arrangement, and Mark had primary custody during the school week because of Carrie's work schedule. Carrie received a promotion and was not able to pick up the kids at her usual times because of work obligations. Mark was supportive of Carrie's new promotion and initially accommodated it because he loved spending time with his kids. The downside was that Carrie was making promises to the kids that she couldn't keep, like fun trips to Disneyland, when she got back into town. During the week, she forgot to FaceTime, as she had promised the kids before bed, because she could not leave her work dinner. Mark felt sad and annoyed for his children. He reached out to Carrie and decided he needed to take the risk and let her know how her actions were affecting the kids. He also would appreciate some consideration, since her work changes were often last minute and forced him to cancel plans that were important to him. Mark shared that Carrie's not following through was making the kids feel sad and not a priority. He also asked her not to make promises that she could not keep. Carrie listened and apologized for her behavior. She felt so anxious about performing well in her new position that she let it get the better of her. Carrie made the commitment to call in the mornings to say hello instead of at nighttime, and she would no longer make sweeping gestures as a way of making the kids happy. Carrie also offered to pay for tutoring at Mark's house to help free him up in the afternoon, since he was the primary caregiver for the kids during the week. Mark accepted Carrie's gesture because he thought the kids could benefit from the help.

Important Points to Consider

Remaining as present as possible with your child is one of the greatest gifts you can offer in parenting. Coparents have the opportunity in shared time to organize their time and to be as available as possible with their child. Here are some suggestions to help you encourage staying present:

○ Quality time with your child is relational and involves meeting your child where he is age-wise. If your child loves to play dinosaurs, then you are going to play dinosaurs.

○ Be cautious of filling your schedule with entertainment as quality time.

○ Response flexibility is a parent's ability to decide how to manage her feelings and thoughts when handling the child. The more response flexibility a parent has, the stronger the ability to think through how you want to handle parenting situations.

○ If you have a coparent who compromises your boundaries, then kindly assert yourself and outline the boundaries you are comfortable with.

 **CHAPTER 15**

Mindfulness in Coparenting

To be a conscious coparent, being mindful in who you are and how you behave around your children is what one might expect. Often, mindfulness and meditation can get confused because they complement each other, but they are two different things. Mindfulness is a state of paying attention to your inner and outer environments, which is something you can practice each day and in the midst of any activity. Meditation is a special practice, a time you set aside to just sit still, breathe, and notice the activity of your mind. One way to think about it is that mindfulness is meditation in motion. Coparents who want to raise children with a sense of being present and available are practicing mindfulness as a living meditation with their families.

Practicing Mindfulness

You do not need to meditate in order to practice mindfulness. However, it can help anchor and deepen your practice. When practicing meditation, you create a simplified environment that is ideally free from the distractions and busyness of life. This makes it much easier to focus and develop mindfulness skills, such as concentration and awareness, which you will need to use back in the chaos of the real world. Think of meditation practice as "going to the gym" for your mind. The foundation and intention that is cultivated during meditation is something you can carry with you everywhere and use in any situation, no matter how stressful.

In recent years, there has been a wealth of scientific research on the effects of mindfulness on the brain. This research has shown the systemic impact that practicing mindfulness has on the brain, as well as specific benefits to both mental health and cognitive functioning. Mindfulness is particularly effective when working with anxiety and depression; it also has a positive impact on attention and executive functioning. Coparenting can at times be anxiety provoking and has the potential for stress. Thus, a mindfulness practice helps to increase one's threshold in handling stress. Research has also shown that the brain is affected both structurally and functionally, meaning that mindfulness can actually stimulate further growth in existing brain cells in specific areas, as well as enhance their existing functionality. This is excellent news for coparents who aim at being highly functional in their parenting and overall lifestyle.

Mood and Emotional Regulation

One of the most powerful impacts of mindfulness practice is on mood. Your mood is influenced by a number of factors, including the amount of certain neurotransmitters circulating through your brain (particularly serotonin), as well as by patterns of brain activity. The brain stem just above the spinal cord produces lots of the brain's serotonin. A joint study by Britta Hölzel and colleagues at the University of Massachusetts Medical Center, Massachusetts General Hospital, and the Justus Liebig University in Germany showed that mindfulness meditation stimulates serotonin synthesis and release in the raphe nuclei.

Serotonin has many functions in the body, but it is closely associated with mood and feelings of happiness and well-being. This may explain one of the ways where mindfulness practice can enhance overall mood and well-being.

Another critical component of mood is the balance of activity between the right and left hemispheres in the region called the prefrontal cortex (PFC). Generally speaking, higher activity on the right side of the PFC is associated with stronger and more frequent negative emotions and a tendency toward avoidance and withdrawal. Conversely, high levels of activity on the left side of the PFC are associated with more positive emotional states and higher levels of flexibility. These patterns apply to reactions to events and to baseline emotional states. A study by Richard Davidson and colleagues at the University of Wisconsin–Madison found that eight weeks of mindfulness training shifted activity in the prefrontal cortex toward the left side of the brain, both as a baseline and in response to stimuli. Participants in the study observed an overall reduction in anxiety, stress, and negative moods. Remarkably, participants maintained this shift even when they were not actively meditating. In the same study, Davidson also observed that mindfulness practice enhanced the ability of practitioners to cool down their emotions when they were stirred up. This is because the prefrontal cortex functions as the conscious control center of the brain, and has the ability to affect functioning in many other parts of the brain. The increase in emotional self-control observed by participants in Davidson's study was a result of a cooling of activity in the amygdala, a structure in the limbic system whose activity closely correlates with negative emotions.

Mindfulness also has a strong impact on rumination, which is one of the most common and difficult to treat symptoms of depression and anxiety. Clinically speaking, rumination is dwelling on negative emotions, thoughts, and memories. It is a passive mental task, one that occurs in the background of the mind and has a tendency to color a person's experiences, putting a negative slant on basically everything that happens. This often appears as withdrawal, where the person who cannot stop ruminating is loath to do much of anything. In a study released in January of 2012, Philipp Keune and his team of researchers at Eberhard Karls University in Germany found that mindfulness is a powerful tool against rumination. It can help reduce rumination over time while also increasing the person's overall activity, which leads to an increased engagement in his life.

INCREASED CONNECTIVITY AND ATTENTION

In a study by UCLA's Lisa Kilpatrick, she and her colleagues found that mindfulness meditation brought about measurable increases in brain connectivity, particularly in the auditory and visual networks. Participants learned that mindfulness improved their ability to maintain focus and block out distractions. One of the strongest effects of mindfulness that Kilpatrick's study found was that not only does mindfulness help you to be less prone to distraction, it actually enhances your ability to focus on what you choose to give your attention to. This also correlates with improved cognitive functioning and perceptual learning, meaning that mindfulness can help you be clearer, sharper, and more focused.

BEING THE PERSON YOU WANT TO BE

One of the most profound benefits of mindfulness is that it can help you to be more like the person you would like to be in the world. One of the first benefits of mindfulness that you (and your child) will see is a heightened awareness of yourself and your inner life, including your emotions, thoughts, and feelings. As you become more aware of these various forces moving within you, you can begin to watch them rise without being at their mercy. For example, when you are aware that you are becoming angry, you have a choice about whether to act on that anger or attend to that feeling directly. Ultimately, mindfulness practice gives you more choices about who you are and how you want to be.

SELF-AWARENESS

The first thing you learn to pay attention to is yourself and the rise of different thoughts and feelings in your own mind. The simple act of noticing that a feeling is coming on, or that a particular idea has come up, can be a powerfully liberating experience.

When you are first starting out, you may not notice that a thought or feeling has taken hold of you until you are in the middle of acting (or after the fact). That is no problem at all. As you become more acquainted with the practice, you will find it easier to notice the movements of your mind as they happen, rather than catching yourself red-handed in the middle of an emotional reaction or outburst (or once it has already passed). You will also start to notice the things that tend to set you off, your triggers, and you will begin to anticipate your emotions before they have a hold on you.

> Your ability to relate to your child involves your capacity for being present. Mindfulness techniques foster a greater capacity for presence. With greater presence comes greater trust between parent and child.

SELF-CONTROL

As you become more skilled at noticing the thoughts and feelings that arise, you will begin to notice them more quickly, maybe even before they start to affect your actions. This awareness is itself a powerful tool. It opens up the possibility to say, "Hey, I'm pretty mad right now," as opposed to yelling at somebody you care about because you were upset about something else. It can do exactly the same thing for your children, helping them learn to communicate about their feelings rather than reacting from that place of emotion. As with most things, children learn this best by seeing it modeled by adults.

Often, you may notice that your emotions carry with them a sense of urgency. As you feel the impulse to do something arise within you, you will be able to see the forces driving that sense of "I need to do something." They could be, for example, the thoughts that come up as you watch your three-year-old put on his shoes. Your mind might be buzzing with impatience, and the thought "I need to put his shoes on for him because he's taking forever" arises. Instead of immediately acting on this thought, you have some room to check in with yourself and act intentionally, instead of just reacting. This practice of noticing creates a certain amount of mental space where you can deal with the thought or feeling itself, rather than acting on it.

Mindfulness is the ability to experience internal attunement. When you can attune to what you are feeling and thinking and demonstrate self-control, you have a stronger capacity for relational integration. Relational integration is the ability to attach and foster healthy connection, embodying mutual understanding, empathy, and validation. Impaired relational integration is linked to impaired neural integration, and that is why it so important to build healthy connections with your children and for you personally. Integrative relationships cultivate the formation of your child's brain and then build self-regulation skills for your child. Positive traits in life are associated with a more integrated brain. Mindfulness increases the interconnectivity of the brain. An integrated brain is the source of optimal self-organization.

Mindfulness author and researcher Jon Kabat-Zinn's research on Mindfulness Based Stress Reduction (MBSR) (used in hospitals and universities throughout the country for chronic pain, depression, and anxiety) showed outcomes correlating to studies on attachment. Secure attachment is external attunement, while mindfulness is internal attunement. Thus, in order for a person to externally attune to others, the ability to internally attune must also happen.

For conscious coparents, mindfulness is the ability to intentionally live in the present moment with your children, and to learn to be present with them even when they are not in your immediate care. Being mindful of your children outside of your care might look like practicing a mindful meditation of your child. Contemplating your child's happiness during prayer or meditation can even feel relaxing for parents. Being mindful outside your immediate care can also be your ability to financially provide healthcare, where you take care of your own health so you can be an active parent. Choosing healthy partners and relationships to be involved in that are supportive of your relationship with your child and your coparent. Being mindful of the kinds of activities that you involve yourself with that support a well-balanced you also supports your coparenting because when you parent you bring all of who you are to the relationship.

If you have a religious faith, many faiths practice contemplative prayer exercises, otherwise known as centering prayer. Selecting a word or short passage of text, and being silent as you allow the word or short passage to permeate your thoughts, will similarly act on the brain the way mindfulness techniques do.

Your ability to live without judgment toward others will also support a stronger presence with your children. Your judgments often get in the way of being fully present because your judgmental thoughts cloud perception. Mindful practice is also about paying attention to the moment without attachment. Trying to control things distracts a person from being in the moment. Carrying mindfulness practice into everyday life changes you as a person. If you find that you do not want to sit and practice mindfulness, then consider mindfulness movements like yoga, dance, martial arts, hiking, tai chi, Qigong, or ritual music making, like drumming. The importance here is to find something that helps you stay mindful so you can foster a deeper presence for yourself and your children.

Relaxation for Coparents

Do you know how to relax, or how to take care of yourself adequately? Many coparents relate to feeling so busy that they don't know how to relax. Their bodies are so keyed up from so much overactivity, that they don't know how to settle down and relax. Relaxation is a key player in adequate self-care. Researcher Jonathan C. Smith looked at how thousands of people described their relaxation responses and came up with twelve basic feelings:

O Physically relaxed

O At ease/peaceful

O Sleepy

O Accepting

O Aware, focused

O Disengaged or neutral

O Optimistic

O Joyful

O Mystery (experiencing insight into profound meaning)

O Quiet

O Reverent and prayerful

O Timeless, boundless, at one

Think about which of these words resonate with you when you feel relaxed. Most coparents may have difficulty setting aside time for themselves because their time away from the kids is work related or spent catching up on life's details, so they can be more available to their children when they have them. If you do not find that you can relate to any of these relaxed feelings, then take the time to evaluate what the roadblocks are that keep you from implementing more relaxation time. At some point, it is not sustainable for you to keep moving at such a fast pace without replenishing. For many women, this type of pace results in autoimmune disorders. For men, heart issues can correlate to stress. Research has shown that the experience of joy and pleasure actually reduces physical inflammation in the body. Therefore, be intentional about incorporating joy and pleasure in each day.

Smith also identifies four categories of relaxation:

O **Basic relaxation:** reducing your physiological response to stress

O **Core mindfulness:** focusing on the world around you while blocking out the constant stream of information secreted by the thought process

O **Positive energy:** awareness of beauty, harmony, happiness, and humor

O **Transcendence:** the recognition of something greater than yourself and a feeling of connection to it

In order to fully relax, you must withdraw from the world mentally, so you can begin a recovery stage. It is in this recovery stage that you open yourself up to receive fulfilling and positive energy from the world within and around you. Conscious coparenting requires focused attention, and your ability to take advantage of downtime, or build in relaxation, will help replenish your fuel tank for your kids when you have shared time with them.

Breath work is a key way to de-stress. Inhaling accesses your sympathetic nervous system, which is the accelerator of the brain. Exhaling accesses your parasympathetic, the brakes of the brain. To foster an effective relaxing breath, make sure your exhale lasts longer than your inhale, giving you more parasympathetic support.

SELF-CARE

In coparenting, you have to identify time that you can set aside for taking adequate care of yourself. Many coparents struggle with setting aside time for fear that it is taking away time from children, work, and responsibilities. It is common for coparents to feel guilty about exercising or taking an hour to read a book or get a massage. These moments can feel like lavish luxuries, and perhaps parents have taken on society's expectations without consciously understanding why.

In terms of your own self-care, how do you intentionally turn off the switch? Evaluating what brings you pleasure and then taking action steps to create it in your life is important. Many parents struggle to think about what things bring them joy outside of the kids. Write down five things that bring you joy or pleasure that do not include your children. Make sure to include things that do not cost money. For example, having a friend over for a cup of coffee to catch up might feel soothing to you. Taking time to pray daily, or journal, might also be a relaxing and joy-filled action step. Regular exercise might be an ongoing action step to stay healthy and manage stress. Once you have identified what needs to happen, take the next step in implementing a schedule to make it happen. Giving yourself an hour a day for some kind of self-care should not be seen as a guilty pleasure, but as properly taking care of yourself for all you are doing. When you model regular self-care to your children, they will see the value in it for themselves when they get older.

BUILD A SUPPORT NETWORK

Having other parents, friends, or hired caregivers who you can ask for help, as well as include in your support network, is also a top self-care strategy. Having a close circle of people who can take turns watching each other's children, help out with errands, and lend moral support is so important when you are a coparent. Hopefully, your coparent will be able to be a part of this network for you, but if not, having others in your circle is even more important.

Important Points to Consider

Mindfulness practice is not just an exercise; it is a way of being. Conscious coparents can use mindfulness to be more fully present with their children and reduce stress. Here are some highlights to keep in mind:

O Relaxation time is key when coparenting. You need time to replenish for all that you are doing and providing for your family.

○ Using simple breath work daily is a form of mindfulness. Use your breath to help de-stress and calm your mind.

○ Evaluate what really soothes you and write down at least five things that you would like to try, or currently do, to take care of yourself.

○ Whatever soothing acts you choose, they also need to put you into a positive mindset.

 **CHAPTER 16**

New Transitions in Coparenting

Coparenting can find its groove after a few years of being mindful in how to work with one another. You will find that when you get it right, it can be a really rewarding experience. Coparenting relationships change when there are major life adjustments for the children. Dynamics in the coparenting relationship have to adjust to the changes too, and this adjustment period can have its share of awkwardness and upsetting moments. If adjusted consciously, it can bring closure to an old chapter and breathe new life into an existing relationship.

Adjusting to New Transitions

Children need time to adjust to new transitions, and many parents make mistakes in not giving their children enough time to process the change. Not giving children enough time to adjust may happen for a few reasons. First, the parent has already made the adjustment and assumes the child has adjusted too. This can be a common theme when parents remarry. The parent is so happy to be remarrying that he assumes that the child will just have to get used to the change. Second, the parent may not want to face what the child is feeling if it is oppositional to how the parent is feeling. Third, parents with older children may feel they are being judged for making changes and become defensive. There may be a fear that the child's upset will threaten the new change in relationship or sibling addition, and take away the parent's new happiness.

If you find yourself resonating with one of these fears, then the solution is to be adequately prepared for the life transition. Children are resilient and they can adapt to new environments, but parents who take the time to make sense of the change help develop their children's resiliency. As a conscious coparent, being mindful that your child needs time to grieve the change is a must. If coparenting is all that your child knows, and then additional relationships come into play with stepsiblings or half-siblings, this is a major change for the child. Understanding your child's fears that accompany the change is crucial because you will know what to attune to. For example, your child may have a fear of being forgotten by you if you are remarrying and having a new baby. Your child might fear that you won't love her as much as you love your new baby. When you identify your child's fears, you can then acknowledge the fear to your child. This attunement helps your child feel "felt" by you. Knowing that you understand builds empathy for what your child is adjusting to, and it will help ease her transition. Let's look at some major coparenting transitions that can affect connection.

REMARRIAGE AND NEW RELATIONSHIPS

When a parent remarries, the child and coparent will have some fears. For the children, having ample time to get to know the fiancé before engagement is ideal. Children need to feel safe with whomever you choose to marry or have a live-in relationship with. If your child does not feel safe, take the time to understand what she is feeling and why. This may be a difficult conversation, but it is a crucial conversation, and understanding your child's perspective may offer insights that you did not see. You will be the mediator between your kids and your new relationship, which has its own share of difficulties.

Remember, whomever you choose to spend your life with means that individual is also spending it with your children. There has to be a mutual chemistry to make things work.

WHEN YOUR CHILD BECOMES A STEPCHILD

Families that include one stepchild and a number of biological children, who are full siblings to one another but only half-siblings to the stepchild, are often the families where a stepchild may feel outnumbered. If your child is being introduced to additional stepsiblings, it is normal that she may not feel that she has the bond her stepsiblings share. She may be the only one who leaves the family unit to visit another entire family, or she may only be with her stepsiblings or half-siblings during visitation. Under these circumstances, visitation times can be challenging. If she lives with half-siblings, she may feel she is missing key family time with her siblings, you, and your partner. If she only visits with her half-siblings, she may feel as though she is perpetually an outsider. If possible, your partner and the other biological parent may want to sit down with her and figure out a visitation schedule where she doesn't feel as though she is missing key events, or that she's not around enough to feel like part of the family.

No matter where your child lives, keep her involved in everything. If you are going to have a family meeting about an upcoming vacation, make sure she is there. If she lives too far away to be there, talk to her on the phone throughout the meeting. If you are planning an event, make sure it is for a day she is available. Keep her informed of everything in the works. The smallest events may feel like big deals to her if she is not able to be there for them. It is the small events that often help make your child feel included. Include your child as often as possible any time that offers family bonding time in the blended family. Remind the extended family to embrace your child as they do their own children. This includes holiday gifts and buying little thoughtful presents during grandparent visits. If you can keep things as equal as possible for all the children in the family, then everyone will feel more included.

The National Stepfamily Resource Center estimates that approximately 65 percent of remarriages include children from at least one of the prior families, and in turn, these remarriages form a stepfamily. Unfortunately, 60 percent of these second marriages will end in divorce. Do not use these statistics as a reason not to consider creating a stepfamily; instead, use them to help you talk with your partner about how you can succeed as a couple and as a stepfamily.

Just as your child needs an adjustment period, your coparent may need a bit of an adjustment period too. Most importantly, outline how your coparenting will continue to work with a new spouse or partner in the picture. Typically, stepparents are the secondary support for the child, not the primary support if you have two coparents who are both available and present for the child. Your stepparent should not be the primary disciplinarian in your household since that is your role as the primary parent. Having a conversation with your new partner and coparent about the expectations you have will help put minds at ease. A meeting for your coparent with the new partner or spouse is helpful because your coparent should know who the major adults in her child's life are. Likewise, it is also helpful for your new partner to have an understanding of how you and your coparent work together. This way a stepparent understands his role as a stepparent and does not initiate changes in what you as coparents have previously decided. Only the coparents should initiate changes. You may take advice from your new spouse, but ultimately decisions for your child are between the two coparents with custody rights.

Research shows that it takes approximately half the years of a child's age for a stepparent to securely attach to a stepchild. For example, if the child is four, then it will take two years to securely attach. If your child is fourteen, then it will take seven years, making your child twenty-one years old by the time the attachment feels complete!

SIBLING ADDITIONS IN NEW MARRIAGES AND COPARENTING

In your new marriage, you can't base your decision to have a child on how your coparent will feel about it. However, the decision will impact your coparent. First and foremost, your coparent will have to deal with any emotions your child feels about the changes. Your child will often confide her feelings with her other parent, rather than the parent who is having another child. Furthermore, a new baby may mean a decrease in resources for your first child, such as time spent at your house, child support, and the role she holds in your family.

You don't need permission to have another child, or even your coparent's blessing; however, you do need to respect your coparent's feelings about the situation and allow time for him to adjust. Instead of letting him find out through the grapevine, from your child, or when your newest addition is born, have a conversation with your coparent to tell him the news. Allow your coparent the freedom to voice his concerns. Outline areas that may impact your coparent, such as a decrease in child support payments, visitation changes, or custody changes. Questions like these are normal and deserve answers, so everyone can be as prepared as possible to better support the situation primarily for your child, and secondarily for the parents.

It is also important to think about the circumstances of your coparent when you decide to tell him you are having another child. Is he remarried? Does he have other biological children with his current partner? Is he able to have more children? Is he still pining away for you? Is the birth of your child going to coincide with any important events he has coming up? Depending on his situation, he might react in different ways. You may know the answers to some of the questions. If he is having trouble having a child with his current partner, you may not know. He may have a surprising reaction and still not tell you the reason; keep these thoughts in the back of your mind. If you do find out that he has an important event around the time of your child's birth, work with him to subdue his concerns. Talk to him about your hope that life will remain as consistent as possible for your child, and let him know that you need his support in order to create a positive experience for your child having a new half-sibling.

Hopefully, you and your new partner will not suffer negative feedback or actions on the part of your coparent. The more respect you can extend to him, the more he may reciprocate. Just like with your child, you may find that your coparent will go through a roller coaster of emotions. Be prepared for some changes in attitude about the pregnancy that may appear to have no rhyme or reason to you or your partner. Remember, the other biological parent may have concerns about his child's well-being, and any erratic behavior by your child may be the result of his concern.

Special Time with Your Child

Children can have a hard time transitioning from sharing their time with just their parent to having to share the time with a stepparent too. Acknowledge this loss of special time or fear of loss. Making sure alone time is made available is important. Similar to living in an intact family, children need one-on-one time away from their siblings so they can soak in being the sole focus of attention with their parent. Typically in coparenting arrangements, there are days on and days off with each parent. Imagine how it might feel for your child to miss you during half the week, and then have to share his time with you for the next three days. Younger children often adapt to this better than older children who have a longer bond with you and may be weary of creating a new bond.

On a weekly basis, plan alone time with your children in the coparenting schedule when you remarry or live with a new partner. Discuss the importance of alone time with your child before getting engaged or living together, so the expectations are understood. Special time can be a couple of hours, like an outing, activity, or dinner out. Having a regularly scheduled special time helps build it into the family's routine. Alone time is uniquely important because it provides the space for the two of you to just be present with each other and nurture your bond. Some special outings with just the stepparent can happen once your child feels comfortable and wants to spend time with just his stepparent. These occasions can really help with building trust and attachment in the stepparent relationship.

If you have reservations about the title stepparent, then consider the more conscious titles of Bonus Mom or Bonus Dad. It's a positive twist on an important relationship that really can enhance your child's development if designed appropriately.

Healthy relationships allow for separate time within reason. Adults who are behaving like adults should not feel threatened by you spending quality time with your child. Setting up vacations, small trips, and outings for just you and your child may be reasonable, provided you discuss them ahead of time, and also make these kinds of outings available to your new spouse too. Your child may also have to adjust to living with other children from your spouse's prior relationship. Tread cautiously on these relationships; understand that children may need an adjustment period. It is common for biological children to feel displaced or jealous of children living regularly in the home of their parent, and who see their parent more than the biological children are able to. Once again, setting aside alone time will help the children feel better and more connected in the relationship with their parent.

HALF-SIBLINGS AND STEPSIBLINGS

The birth of a new half-sibling can be a mix of joy and fear for a child. Just as children in intact homes may fear the birth of a new sibling and question how much love and attention will be available, this fear is intensified in coparenting relationships when remarriage occurs and a new family begins. The half-sibling represents the creation of a new intact family, and your child from your previous relationship may feel replaced and/or fear there is no room for him. Make sure to alleviate any worries that you will have a favorite child, or that you are replacing the connection you have with your child. If your child has had a secure connection with the stepparent, the birth of a sibling can be a rupture in the connection if the child questions if the stepparent will love her the same way as the biological child. Wise stepparents have the opportunity to set in motion the idea that the birth of the new child actually represents a familial connection for the whole family. Demonstrating impartial love and attention from both the parent and stepparent will continue to help foster the relationship.

Coparent Reactions to Transitions

If you are a coparent who is adapting to your child having a stepparent, you may also struggle with feelings of being replaced. It is normal to feel this way. Remember, your child's primary bond is with you as her mom or dad, and that is irreplaceable. If your child comes to you to process her feelings about her parent's new marriage or living arrangement, be as empathic as you can. Listen to her feelings and communicate to your child, sharing with her other parent as well. You may need to bring up your child's concerns if your child asks for help, or if your child is too small to verbalize. Honor her confidentiality, unless, of course, your child is being hurt. The primary person you still need to speak with about your child is your fellow coparent. If you find that your child's stepparent is intruding into conversations that are between you and your coparent, then bring it to your coparent's attention that the two of you need to agree on issues concerning your child. Over the course of years, and due to trust that is built with stepparents, the ability to speak with stepparents may change.

Bonus parents have the opportunity to love and support the child. As Hillary Clinton has often been quoted, "It takes a village to raise a child." See bonus parents as part of your child's village. The more supportive and safe individuals your child has in her community, the better your child is for it. It can be common in really thriving stepparenting relationships that by the teen years, the stepparent can be a safe sounding board for the teen when the primary parents are not allowed access. Give bonus parents the benefit of the doubt and take your cues on how they are doing as bonus parents based on how your children are feeling and thinking about the relationship.

MOVING

Dealing with a job relocation, or deciding to move, after you have been coparenting in the same area can be very difficult for your child to adjust to. It is a loss for both of you, your child and your coparent, if you have to move a great distance that changes the visitation arrangement because a system was in place, and that system is now influx. Preparing your coparent for the changes, and figuring out a schedule that works for both of you, will be very important. You will need to document the changes. Child support may also need to be adjusted. Once you figure out the schedule changes with your coparent, tell your child what is about to happen. Your child will go through a grieving process, but this can be supported by any adjustments you can make to ensure that you can be regularly available by Skype for things like homework assistance, daily calls, frequent trips to visit, and planning to be available for special events for your child whenever possible.

OVERPROTECTING CHILDREN

It is common for coparents to be anxious about their children handling discomfort and disappointment, especially after a major life transition, and feel the need to save their child from potentially experiencing these feelings or further feelings of hurt. However, overprotection inadvertently teaches children that Mom or Dad thinks, "I can't handle problems or survive disappointment. I need others to take care of me." If the goal as parents is to raise children who become self-corrective adults, then we must allow children the opportunity to think through problems on their own and try new things.

Rather than trying to prevent these transitions from happening, think about how you want to be available as a parent to help your child make sense of the transition. Remember, your child will get her cues about how to handle the transition based on how you are handling it. Making sure you are available and following through on commitments you have made to your child will help smooth the transition. For example, if you have a standing Daddy/Daughter Date Night, keep the ritual even after you remarry. These kinds of rituals often mean a great deal to your children.

Taking on too much responsibility in your coparenting, and not sharing enough power with your coparent or delegating age appropriate chores for your child, can also derail the formation of a healthy self-esteem. Examples of this might be if you are the type of parent who makes your child's lunch at ten years old, cleans the whole house, including your child's bedroom, and/or feeds all the animals in the house for the sake of saving time because your child is too slow. Your child's dependency might make you feel important, or may be annoying, but relinquishing some of the control and delegating jobs at home that are age appropriate is helpful and respectful of your child's development.

Important Points to Consider

Coparenting can go through several adjustments. Just as you adjust to the developmental stages of your child, you and your coparent may also be personally developing through remarriage or births of additional half-sibling and/or stepsiblings. Here are some additional considerations:

- O Give your child time to adjust to the new transition of a remarriage or additional siblings. Do your best to be as available as possible and don't forget your child's feelings.

- O Children need to feel safe with whomever you choose to marry or have a live-in relationship with.

- O Work with your coparent on setting the boundaries for stepparents in your parenting arrangement. Outline the expectations you have for the stepparent, so she can be set up for success as your child's bonus parent.

- O Make sure to continue special time with your child if you remarry or have additional children.

Index